THE WHO YOU DREAM
YOURSELF

THE WHO YOU DREAM YOURSELF

Playing and Interpretation in Psychotherapy and Theatre

Val Richards

KARNAC

LONDON   NEW YORK

First published in 2005 by
H. Karnac (Books) Ltd.
6 Pembroke Buildings, London NW10 6RE

British Library Cataloguing in Publication Data

A C.I.P. for this book is available from the British Library

  ISBN 1 85575 313 8

Edited, designed and produced by The Studio Publishing Services Ltd, Exeter EX4 8JN

Printed in Great Britain by Hobbs the Printers Ltd, Totton, Hampshire

10 9 8 7 6 5 4 3 2 1

www.karnacbooks.com

CONTENTS

CHAPTER SEVENTEEN

CHAPTER EIGHTEEN

"quem te sonhas"
("The who you dream yourself")
from: "Advice", by Fernando Pessoa

ACKNOWLEDGEMENTS

My particular thanks to the following for their rigourous scrutiny of early drafts and their most constructive advice: Gay Crace, Jane Lindsay, and John Rowe.

Thanks also to Stephen Friedrich, Veronica Norburn, Sue Rumney, Mia Rawal, and Maria Schleger for specific material; also to fellow patients, colleagues, and trainees who have caused this book to exist.

With gratitude to the Squiggle Foundation, especially Nina Farhi, who first provided the time and the place.

Thanks also to Karnac and to the cover artist, Robert J. Railton.

I should point out that details of original identity for all who feature in the following pages have been disguised.

ABOUT THE AUTHOR

Val Richards was previously a teacher of English and Drama. She is a therapist, a supervisor, and a seminar leader for trainees. At her placement in a psychiatric hospital, she introduced a popular drama therapy group; she also established a project on Winnicott for Islington playworkers. She is a former Assistant Director of the Squiggle Foundation and she edited two monographs for the Winnicott Studies Monograph series, *The Person Who is Me* (Karnac, 1996) and *Fathers, Families and the Outside World* (Karnac, 1997). Her publications include "His Majesty, the baby", in *Shakespeare and the Changing Curriculum* (edited by Wheale and Ayres, Routledge, 1991), "Time-sickness" (1993) and "Mothers, mirrors and masks" (1994), in *Winnicott Studies*, "Article" in *Revista Chilena de Psicoanalisis* 16, December 1999, and "Winnicott and education", in *The Ship of Thought: Essays on Psychoanalysis and Learning* (edited by Duncan Barford, Karnac, 2002).

Preface

Part one: signs and spaces

The motif of space and time running through this book builds on Winnicott's evocation of playing to focus in Part One on the work-ings of language and meaning-making in the settings of infancy, therapy, and theatre.

Part two: the struggle between masks

Gaps between thought and speech imply gaps between self and representations of self, for which the metaphor of masks is invoked. Masks are seen as an integral part of the personality, facing both inward and outwards, protecting the "core of the personality which never communicates with the world of perceived objects" (Winnicott, (1965, p. 187). This section is concerned with the role of masks, both inner and outer, in contributing to the necessary space within the personality and between self and others.

As a modification of Winnicott's True/False Self dichotomy, I consider how the phenomenon of theatrical "forced masks and free masks" serves as an analogy for the range of positions inadequately covered by the True and False Self umbrella.

Part three: signs and times

Space and linear time are one and indivisible. Disturbance in one means disturbance in the other. In the relationship between self and time "Good time" is linked to creativity, implying a balanced relationship between present, past, and future, with asleep dreaming a vital accompaniment. "Bad time" or Time Sickness suggests alienation, an excessive distance from one's home in the present. To feel "real" depends on being now as well as being here. In precipitating "nowness", the work of therapy contends with the seductive fantasy that *other* times—past and future—are more real than being here, today.

Introduction

At the time of beginning my own therapy, I was teaching drama and theatre studies and became fascinated by the analogies between theatre and therapy, especially by how these set-apart space–times affect the behaviour of meaning-making and the seeming immensity of the therapist's power.

The therapy room, the garden just glimpsed through the window, and even the park beyond, were all extensions of the therapist herself, all transformed into special and exciting spaces. As for time and clock watching, I jealously guarded each second of the allotted fifty minutes and raged at being kept waiting outside after the appointed starting time. The strangeness of this actual space and time was reflected also by upheavals of inner spaces and inner times.

Then, as a trainee psychotherapist discovering the writings of Winnicott, I realized that his theory of transitional phenomena and his vision of *"playing"*, which is *exciting and "has a place and a time"* (Winnicott, 1971, p. 41), provided a theoretical underpinning to the bond between theatre and therapy, bringing together the three parts of this book.

As a unifying metaphor for both theatre and therapy, *playing* seemed also to modify the supposed therapist–patient missionary position. Winnicott's locating the therapist more "alongside" than "above" the patient, with the metaphor of therapist and patient in an overlapping space, *playing* together and separately, was liberating. Winnicott's concept of playing, with its highly specific connotations, led me to draw a provisional distinction between "playing" and "games", which is modified at the end of the book.

For me, Winnicott's concept of playing in therapy appeared to lessen that inequality which arises from the dynamic between petitioner and petitioned in any formal situation. But it is further cranked up in therapy by the classic stance of therapist as chief interpreter of very vulnerable soul-barers. It was ironical, therefore, that my therapist, who appeared to me in such an Olympian light, would, I think, also herself subscribe to Winnicott's vision of playing between therapist and patient. Here was a tangle of fantasies and projections demanding to be unravelled.

Part of this tangle belonged to confusions of identity, heightened by the intensification of feelings and meaning-making in this set-apart space and time. Winnicott's ideas of the Self, "the person who is me" (Winnicott, 1989, p. 271) and the 'True and False Self' (Richards, 1996, p. 7) I found magnetic. I remember my therapist's eloquent silence when I asked her to tell me which of the various psychoanalytic models of the self she, personally, espoused.

I found that Winnicott's ideas of the self were supplemented and illuminated by those of Jung, who viewed the "persona", or social mask, as an integral part of the psyche with no connotations of falseness. This linked with the function of theatrical masks and, especially, their portrayal in the prose, drama, and poetry of W. B. Yeats.

For Yeats, also, masks are essential to the self: potentially liberating and free, or potentially constricting and forced. Here the writings of Lacan play a vital role, in his implication that perhaps there are *only* masks since the perceived self/ego is based on a mistake, a delusion, with mirrors more related to gazing than to reflecting.

As this book neared completion, I was getting the impression that the dialectic between masks and selves had become reflected and played out in my overall text, that the pages were haunted by two fundamentally opposed kinds of personality. At first, the difference of type looked like the contrast between observer and observed. But that could not be quite right, since the person who feels most pierced by the eyes of others must also be the person who is most watchful and wary in guarding against the other's gaze—the observed is the mother of all observers.

Then, fortuitously, the following passage from a recent novel leapt off the page, reminding me of the obvious: that the mother of all observers is the observer of *herself*:

> . . . He [Christopher] loved the energy of the city, the utter lack of self-consciousness. The trouble was, he couldn't let himself go. He felt as if he were an onlooker at his own life, watching his actions from a distance. At this moment he was a father having quality time with his daughter—over-reacting, over enthusiastic, his voice booming with false bonhomie. He could see it was a beautiful autumn day—foliage on fire, the twin spires of the San Remo building rearing into the sky—but all he was thinking was how to describe it later to show [his wife] Marcia he had noticed. [Moggach, 2004, p. 135]

The extract captures the disturbed narcissism, the navel-gazing and inner division of a contemporary western consciousness torn in two by the weight of its own self-awareness. Christopher is divorced from himself, so he cannot properly *experience* the acknowledged glory of the autumn day. This exhaustion of self-consciousness is contrasted (not for the first time in fiction), by Christopher and other characters in the novel, with the seemingly rich, instinctual spontaneity of those who are among the most poor—Indians, in this case.

Christopher's stream-of-consciousness here displays further how such excessive self-observation prevents the possibility of being fully *here, now*, which is a main theme of this book. Because "he couldn't let himself go", Christopher is "watching his actions from a distance", having largely absconded from the present and flown ahead to the future, the next big thing, of reporting to his wife this experience that was happening now: "but all he was thinking was how to describe it later to show Marcia he had noticed". For Christopher, the unity of his being in time and space is disrupted.

In terms of Winnicott's playing metaphor, this self-alienation in time and space means that Christopher is unable to live creatively, to play. For playing happens from the depths of the personality and depends on the unity of self in space and time and on a capacity for imagination as well as dreaming while asleep—then you *can* "let yourself go". All these qualities appear as essential for creative meaning-making and symbolic activity. But Christopher is engaged in that aspect of meaning-making called *fantasy* or day-dreaming, which fares less well in Winnicott's line-up of favourable qualities. Fantasy and day-dreaming are associated with a "split-off" or dissociated part of the self, embodied neither in real time nor space. (This will be taken up in Part Three, Chapter 12.)

But once actually in India, Christopher is wholly there. Paralysing fantasy turns into live imagination. His sluggish feelings are revived by the attentions of a gorgeous temple goddess and, however briefly, he comes together as a whole personality. For me, while refreshing my sense of clear oppositions *between* types of personality, the novel jogged my realization that within the *same* skin the polarized types are jostling and jousting. And it should not have needed the further fortunes of this character, Christopher, to tell me that splits within the *same* person can mend, or at least be splinted. Things move from sterile gazing to live reflecting, from half-hearted presence and withdrawal to openness and spontaneous self-expression, from games to playing—and back again.

Thus, while the theoretical human being behind the portrayal of language and meaning-making in Chapter One may well accord in some respects to the wary, guarded type of speaker, this may equally be the same speaker who, in Chapter Five, excels at freedom of association. For, as described in Chapter One, both aspects are a universal property of symbolic activity.

PART I

SIGNS AND SPACES

"Playing has a place and a time. It is not inside by any use of the word . . . Nor is it outside, that is to say it is not part of the repudiated world, the not-me, that which the individual has decided to recognise (with whatever difficulty and even pain) as truly external, which is outside magical control"

(Winnicott, 1971, p. 41).

In everyday life, "if" is a fiction, in the theatre "if" is an experiment.
In everyday life, "if" is an evasion, in the theatre "if" is the truth.
When we are persuaded to believe in this truth, then the theatre and life are one.
This is a high aim. It sounds like hard work.
To play needs much work. But when we experience the work as play, then it is not work any more.
A play is a play.

(Brook, 1968, p. 157)

CHAPTER ONE

Language, space, and meaning-making

"Die Sprache spricht" ("Language speaks Man")

(Heidegger, quoted in Leavy, 1983, p. 7)

"The peasant said he wasn't surprised that astronomers, with all their instruments could figure out the size of the stars and their course—what baffled him was how they found out their names"

(Vygotsky, 1934, p. 222)

"Inner speech is speech for oneself; external speech is for others"

(Vygotsky, 1934, p. 225)

Winnicott's vision of an original "time and place for play-ing" between baby and m/other equates playing with the development of meaning-making, with the capacity for symbolization. A "time and a place" appear not simply as the background to this playing. They are prime actors in the drama of symbolic mastery, the individual's discovery that, as affirmed by Jacques Rousseau, "how pleasant it is . . . to move the world simply by moving the tongue" (Culler, 1983, p. 104).

Adult reconstructions of infant experience suggest that the early playing between m/other and baby is experimental, risky, marking the infant's gradual progression from its own omnipotent "creation" of the world to the full powers of mental and cultural life. One minute the infant is absorbed in its teddy bear or other favoured object and the next, he or she may be startled into sensing that the nearby m/other is a someone else, and not after all an indivisible part of him or herself. Now, if the mother disappears from view, the baby starts to cry. Not only is this mother "irrevocably" lost, but perhaps the baby may also be terrified that part of himself has vanished. He does not yet have either a full sense of himself in his own separate skin in space or a strong enough awareness of "going-on-being" in time. Feelings of loss and of being torn apart are made worse because only *this* moment is real, stretching on without end. There is still no concept of "in a minute" or "soon" mother will come back.

The immense leap to the realization, "Mother did come back before, so she will come back again" is an embryonic thought—or the precursor of a thought. It is enabled by the baby's now retaining an inner image of the mother and thus starting to link up moments in time. He learns to picture a future moment and remember a past moment. Sooner or later, he no longer howls if the mother disappears. Instead of existing only in disconnected moments, he starts to experience time as more joined up and himself as bounded by his own skin, held in time and space.

The discovery of otherness and, therefore, of self in a special time and a place for playing thus involves a rhythm of separating and merging between mother and child. It is this transitional, fluid state that is seen as the source and basis of further creative, cultural, and artistic activity. Metaphorical, imaginary space/times for playing open up into the actual spaces of therapy, theatre, and other "acts apart".

The basic conditions of these: the ritual of an appointed time and place for meeting plus, traditionally, an agreed fee, forge both a bond and a barrier between the protagonists. In the glare of set-apart times and spaces, whatever happens, every detail, every word, may acquire a special, heightened significance. Here, illusion and reality intermingle and also contend for the upper hand. The patient in therapy, like the theatre spectator, is caught in a willing suspension of disbelief, while simultaneously knowing that what is unfolding is partly illusory—that on the stroke of midnight, s/he must return, with no fuss, to her/his outside, everyday world. The secret of survival in these times and spaces lies in managing to sustain a tension between illusion and reality, without loss to either; but the patient for whom the seeming *reality* of the analytic experience eclipses its illusory, its token, aspect, may silently keep these things in his or her heart.

The patient is simultaneously reading and interpreting his/her therapist's behaviour and if the therapist is aware of this continual parallel activity the imagined gulf between patient and therapist narrows. Such narrowing contributes to a shift in the focus of psychotherapy away from "interpretation" by the therapist of the patient's material towards playing, both together and apart. For "playing" implies that the child/patient's own interpreting and self-communing is no less busy than the mother/therapist's. Child and m/other play together and the child also plays alone in the m/other's presence.

What is going on? What are these players up to in the separate musings and silences that punctuate their meetings? Patients are easily distressed and panicked by silences, whether the therapist's staring presence seems to be engulfing or whether his/her silence means s/he has deserted them. One patient, after a lively discussion of a dream about rose gardens, was unable then to endure a —to her—agonizing silence that signalled the analyst's disappearance, but was helped by his saying, "Why can't I be in my garden and you be in your garden?"

Apart from assumed *unconscious* activity, the scene of shared and separate playing is a reminder of the gaps that exist between conscious thought and its expression. Such gaps reflect the primary function of symbolic activity: communication to oneself in making sense of our experience of the world.

Beyond the buzz of silence and speech in the settings of infancy, therapy, and theatre, this pattern of dual mental activity reflects theories of the symbolic which prioritize the *inner* function of verbal language above its commonly emphasized role as vocal expression and outer communication. As will emerge in this chapter, spaces, degrees of distance, determine the behaviour of words, of verbal language both in the perceived relationship between name and named and between self and other.

Drawing on contemporary philosophical and structuralist–post-structuralist ideas, this chapter relates key features of language (the symbolic) specifically to the Talking Cure—to the negotiated space between patient and therapist.

Emotional and psychological disturbance brings a narrowing of the space between symbol and symbolized, which is paralleled by a narrowing of the space between patient and therapist. The thinning of this gap between symbol and symbolized is defined as "symbolic equation", where both difference and similarity get swallowed up by sameness. Symbolic equation entails the loss—however briefly—of the "as if" metaphorical dimension.

The specific features of language that bear directly on the Talking Cure and shed light on its disruption include the following.

(1) *The view that one's perception of the world is subject to a specifically inherited symbolic order.*

According to twentieth century linguists, language both liberates and limits. Whatever tongues we are first exposed to *determines* our perception of reality. We experience the world according to the linguistic categories we inherit. "Language speaks Man" (Heidegger, p. 7) This accords with the Lacanian view that we are inscribed into a specific symbolic order, shaping us even before birth (see Chapter Two).

The most commonly mentioned, (possibly now discredited) example of differing carve-ups of reality in specific cultures is the Inuits' twenty-two different names for snow, in contrast to our three or four. Of course, it is not hard to imagine how lives that revolve around snow would throw up a range of "snowy" situations demanding definition. These could be related to colour, shape, weight, texture—from treacherous wetness to light dryness, etc.

Consider, similarly, how the therapist's perception of his or her patients may be shaped by the prior diagnostic categories of, say, "borderline"/"schizoid"/"schizophrenic", "narcissistic", "hysterical". Once the reality of a patient has been divided into a certain spectrum of pathological classifications, the patient then tends to meet imagined expectations of belonging to one of those categories. One recent example of this is the noticeable increase in cases of multiple personality following its portrayal in certain well publicized books and films. This does not demonstrate whether these cases were real or phoney, but that they seemed to require a prior conceptualization in order to "come out", or even to materialize into existence at all.

But whatever dividing up of reality we absorb from our particular culture, we could not, without words, without a system of signs, make sense of our experience; we could not define or think about it. We could not create and recreate the world for ourselves in all the cultural activity that issues from primary symbolic achievement, and we would lack the capacity productively to relate past, present, and future on which all civilization depends. As elaborated in Chapters Two and Three and in Section Three, "Signs and times", the operation of individual time and space and the possession of language are inseparable.

So, while on the one hand our perception is constrained by those lenses that we inherit, on the other hand, as expounded by the philosopher Suzanne Langer (Langer, 1942, p. 44), words, because they bear no resemblance to their subject, are the most advanced form of symbolization available to us. Unspoken or spoken to another, their inexhaustibility confers infinite power.

(2) *Interpretation—meaning-making—takes precedence over communication.*

Of primary concern to psychotherapy, therefore, is the insistence that above and prior to the function of language as *communication* with others, is the role of language as our *chief means of representing reality* to *ourselves*. While it is true that this function is bound up with other persons and so involves communication, it is seen as imperative to grasp the primacy of one's own and others' inner relationship to language. In psychoanalytic thought, much is made of the intermingling of your internalized picture of another with the actuality of that person. Whom you communicate with in the world is the Who who has been filtered through your dreams, your fantasy, your "projections".

It is, I believe, this inner, representational aspect of language above its use for communication with others that is especially relevant to the paradox of the Talking Cure, where, in fact, what is spoken aloud to the therapist turns out to be only the tip of the iceberg. Simultaneously, alongside that talking, a silent "representing the world to oneself" proceeds in the form of a private dialogue.

This privileging of language for inner self-communing above language for speaking with others ensures a contradiction at the heart of analytic practice, when the therapist asks you to express aloud whatever comes into your mind.

Such a request assumes that "you" are an entity rather than— for many people—the duo comprising the "you" who might first need to run your thoughts past that "you" who is cocking an attentive ear before letting you express them to the analyst.

It might also be that, ironically, the division between inner, interpreting self and outer, speaking-aloud self is compounded by the seemingly unavoidable elevation of the therapist and the consequent concern about the impact of one's words upon him or her. The fostering of the transference intended to elicit trust and freedom of expression might result in greater inhibition, for the therapist, rather than the patient, might seem to get placed at the centre of operations.

A therapist's awareness of the patient's parallel, largely private activity alongside the shared participation and communication, prepares him or her for signs of the therapy breaking down. This activity is not to be equated with what might be designated the patient's *unconscious* processes; we are looking at a more than half-conscious activity.

(3) *Language, the most arbitrary and flexible form of symbolization.*

Also relevant to psychotherapy are those defining qualities that constitute words as the supreme form of symbolization. Like the therapeutic contract itself, words exist and endure solely by consensus and convention. Only if those belonging to the particular group or society come to adopt, say, the name "dog" for this animal will that name survive.

The consensual, provisional nature of naming ensures that words are both *arbitrary* and *flexible*. These qualities confer supremacy on verbal language as the most advanced form of symbolization. Arbitrariness and flexibility imply two things. Because there is no intrinsic, essential link between word and meaning, between signifier and signified, we can picture a gap between them. Meaning is constituted partly by this space between word and meaning and thus by the *difference* between one word and another.

A word does not have any "natural" relationship with what it names. It just differs from other words. Even in the case of certain onomatopaeic words, the alleged similarity is usually dubious: the name of an object does not reflect its property.

The "sign" born of the union between word and meaning is therefore precarious, loosely connected, gaping, unstable. For word and meaning are not truly, tightly bonded like the two sides of one sheet of paper, as originally claimed by the structuralist, Saussure, 1857–1913 (in Sturrock, 1982, pp. 6–7).

Thus, secondly, because the relationship between word and meaning is arbitrary, existing only by convention, by cultural/social consensus, words possess the *flexibility* of potentially infinite combinations of letters. In the dictionary sense, you can make any combination of letters mean anything at all, as long as others accept your chosen definition.

These features of arbitrariness and flexibility in language are the primary source of its inexhaustibility and its infinite power as a human tool. Indeed, I consider that the maxim, "Sticks and stones / may break my bones / But words will never hurt me" is most blatantly false.

No less vital is allowing for the fact that the meaning of a spoken word and of strings of spoken words depends not only on convention, but also on *context*. For the same word can mean entirely different or opposite things. Depending on its context, for example, "swallow" can refer to a beautiful bird or to the action of making food go down your throat. The word "cleave" signifies either "to unite" or "to sever". Clearly, only context can convey how it is being used. However, for ambiguities, contradictory messages, emotional overtones and undertones, all the rhetorical devices of tone and style come into play. Then context extends beyond the words spoken to include the total emotional atmosphere in all its variations. I would suggest that much of what ensues in this book is indebted to the widespread movement in psychoanalytic practice towards placing overall context above content in the relationship between therapist and patient.

(4) *Symbolic equation as a natural part of symbolic development.*

The essential arbitrariness and looseness of connection between word and meaning exist despite the fact that mental capacity, originating in early life, depends utterly on the illusion of a seeming inseparability, a "no-space" between name and named, for a child's grasp of the arbitrary relationship between words and meanings is slow to mature. (This will be seen, in Chapter Eleven, as relevant to disturbance and regression in psychotherapy.)

In the minds of young children, words and meanings are fused together by an imagined identity or equivalence. Tests by such psychologists as Piaget and Vygotsky, asking young children, "Why is a cow called a cow?" produced the reply, "Because it has horns", and in response to "Why is ink called ink?" they reasoned, "Because it is black" (Vygotsky, 1934, p. 222). Similarly, in earlier times and primitive societies, the "true" name of a person equalled that person. There was a "no-space" between name and meaning, signifier and signified. Possession of a person's "true" name gave you total power over him or her.

This mode of thought, a form of symbolic equation, as mentioned above, is a natural developmental stage from which, other things being equal, the child will emerge. But traces or elements of such a concrete way of experiencing words and meaning also linger in everyday adult life—to its enrichment or as an expression of disturbance.

For example, many people, despite the *essential* emptiness/ featurelessness of all words, feel that names of many kinds have particular colours. This seems to apply especially to the names of people, months, and days of the week.

When words are combined into particular patterns of sound and rhythm, alliteration and assonance, to make rhymes and poems, these seem to become palpable, tangible things, artefacts, to treasure and repeat. Slogans and homely folk sayings soothe and support, while spells and incantations are ascribed dynamic power. Special code words arise from a particular context between patient and therapist, which possess a life, a solidity of their own that belies the fundamental nature of the medium.

Apart from such enriching ways with language that apparently derive from original immature reasoning, in adulthood the concept of a space between symbol and symbolized and between one subject and another is, for the most part, unthinkingly taken for granted.

(5) *A narrowing of the space in the relationship between name and named, word and meaning, signalling symbolic equation and psychological disturbance.*

The disruption of this relationship between symbol and symbolized will be considered in Chapter Ten, "No-space, regression and symbolic equation". A narrowing of the space between symbol and symbolized may be paralleled by a narrowing of the space between patient and therapist. The thinning of this gap between symbol and symbolized is seen as a pathological form of "symbolic equation", where both difference and similarity get swallowed up in *sameness*. This form of symbolic equation entails the losing—however briefly—of the "as if", metaphorical dimension of one's experience.

CHAPTER TWO

The genesis of meaning-making

I n acknowledging the link between adult psychotherapy, infancy, and early childhood, it is necessary also to observe that what happens to meaning-making between adults in the analytic space directly contributes to and influences theories and assumptions about infant states. For a big feature in psychoanalytic theories of infant development and of the nature of the self is their basis in *adult* roots, from the shoots that spring up in clinical work with adults. Just as direct experience with babies and children, through infant observation and actual parental experience, influence psychotherapy, so also, psychotherapy with adults contributes to and shapes the myths and maps of infancy.

There is a recursive element, a loop: for these myths and maps of babyhood, which in part originate *from* work with adults, are then applied as a template *for* adults. Reductive infantile readings of adults may thus mask a prior recycling for infants of *adult* material.

Such material, therefore, may sometimes be saying as much as— or more—about the complexity of adulthood than about its roots in infancy. The parallels may imply no less that "adults are like babies" than that "babies are like adults"—or are imagined to be like them. Only consider, for example, the rapturous meditations from an adult perspective by analytic writers on the infant's feelings towards the breast (e.g., Meltzer, Bion, Benvenuto). So, the apparent naturalness of the analogy between therapist–patient and mother–baby may suppress some of their dissimilarity. Hence, this dialectic is a two-way affair. As much as regressive manifestations by adults seem to reflect early life, this view of "early life" is itself partly constructed from observation of *adult* complexities.

Especially in Winnicott's inspired portrayal of infant development, an overlap is reflected in the interplay between his long-term work with actual babies and his experience of the original "infant" in his adult patients. It was the latter, he claimed, who taught him most about early life. For him, this "child" of the imagination was no less real than an actual child patient.

The mirror and the sound of meaning

A central metaphor for early meaning-making and a precursor of playing, for Winnicott, is the "mirroring" between mother and infant. For Winnicott, not just the eyes alone, but the mother's whole *face* does the mirroring that gives the baby meaning. Whatever noisy interplay is going on at the same time is left to our imagination. The visual is here the primary sense, standing also for holding, touch, and even for sound in this complex mutual communication:

> "What does the baby see when he or she looks at the mother's face?" he asks, replying, 'I am suggesting that, ordinarily, what the baby sees is him or her self. In other words, the mother is looking at the baby *and what she looks like is related to what she sees there.* [Winnicott, 1971, p. 112, original italics]

This scenario suggests that the reflection of itself that the infant receives and is sustained by is totally dependent on the image of another—the expression on the mother's face. Far from appearing as an over-and-done-with instant, her affirmation appears as a process. For this baby to see itself involves a sequence, a chronology. The *mother* must first see the child and respond to what she sees, so that as the child looks at the mother, he sees himself, already there. It is a benign cycle in which the mother is repeatedly giving the infant back to himself.

With the mother's repeated affirmation of her infant separate sensations become more joined up, less fragmented. Reliable mirroring launches the child on the road to meaning-making, as he or she begins to experience "going-on-being" (Winnicott, 1965, p. 47) in time and space. It is through such "finding one's self in the other" (Fonagy, 1995) that the self is strengthened.

Winnicott's mirroring scene contrasts with the accounts of Freud and Lacan of the infant's dawning self-awareness. Lacan first construed the mirror stage more in terms of a solipsistic moment, with no one else involved. Like Narcissus, by means of its own image alone the infant graduates to the sense of itself. For both Freud and Lacan the step could be formulated as: "it takes one plus nought to make one", whereas for Winnicott, it takes "one *plus one* to make one".

The absorbed communion of Winnicott's seemingly silent mirroring scene is a symbolic reminder that, for him, not only is the sense of seeing and being seen paramount but also sounds and words appear to be secondary, of less importance than other modes of communication.

> What is the answer? Shall we stop trying to understand human beings? The answer might come from mothers who do not communicate with their infants except in so far as they are subjective objects. By the time mothers become objectively perceived their infants have become masters of various techniques for indirect communication, the most obvious of which is the use of language. [Winnicott, 1965, p. 188]

Four hands clapping

If Winnicott's treatment of early infant experience stresses seeing and being seen, in Lacanian writings, the emphasis is on hearing and being heard.

> Before the child is born and sometimes even before its conception, before it cries or speaks, it is spoken about. There is already

alienation; something of the parents is already there that will mark the child if it comes to be born. [Faladé, 1987, p. 49]

This belief is dramatized in a haunting account by the contemporary Lacanian, Catherine Mathelin, where the analyst seems magically to treat and cure a ceaselessly crying three-month-old infant, Cannelle, by "holding" and "mirroring" her with words, seemingly more than with visual communication. Not sounds alone, but the words and meaning, the narrative pattern of the analyst's words, were allegedly decisive. As the analyst talked continually to the baby, she was painstakingly unravelling the tangled skeins of the mother's story and the baby's story, reclaiming for Cannelle the identity that had been sucked into the mother's own. The whole accent is on sound, "saying", "crying", "hearing", "making noise", "new voice", "swallowing" words:

> C.M: So Cannelle, you hear what mother and father are saying? You've been crying ever since you came out of mother's tummy, ever since you've been able to make noise, as if you were afraid noone would remember that you exist. But you're there. [Mathelin, 1999, pp. 159–160]

Then, apparently, Cannelle stopped crying and gazed at the therapist, while the mother began crying silently. The therapist assured Cannelle that she need not be afraid, that she *could* sleep and that mother also would be able to sleep. Mathelin claims that this "new voice" gave Cannelle an "alternative path". She "seemed to swallow the analyst's words with her whole body" . . . and "suddenly the child's eyes turned up, her fists opened—and Cannelle fell asleep in her mother's arms for the very first time". When she "seemed to swallow the analyst's words with her whole body" it is as if her entire being became mouth and ears.

Cannelle's transformation might be explained by the altered dynamics caused by the intervention of the analyst and by the mother's beginning to relax, as the co-recipient of the therapist's words. The music of pure sound alone might also be effective for the distressed baby. But this writer nevertheless insists that it is the *meaning* of the words that is decisive in Cannelle's recovery.

This rests on Lacan's claim that, unlike Winnicott's picture of early mother–infant oneness, even from the outset mother and infant are never merged, that "there is no mother–infant symbiosis, since from the outset there is a third term, a lack on the basis of which all interaction is organised" (Lacan, 1975, p. 152). So there is always a lack which constitutes a space for the symbolic, for meaning-making. Far from experiencing an undifferentiated bliss as it starts to suck, the baby may well feel the breast is only second best, for in the act of birth the baby has been torn from itself. There has always been a gap between baby and m/other, a lack of wholeness.

In other words, in this scenario, there is *always*, psychologically, time and space between mother and baby. The "lack from the outset" coming from the insertion of the symbolic, of language between the "I" and the "self". is the perpetual wound of the symbolic, of a cultural inheritance determined by the word, which "was in the beginning" and by which "all things were made".

In the case of Cannelle, what seems to count beyond mere words is hearing and feeling the *presence* of organized meaning, as mediated by the analyst's authority and power. Perhaps, even in early life, there is more music in the presence of intended *meaning* than in sounds alone or in pure gobbledygook. For the psychotherapy patient, the primacy attached to hearing the meaning-laden sounds could accord with Bollas's reference to the times when the sound of the analyst's voice (Bollas, 1987, p. 21) matters above the expressed meanings. It also echoes T. S. Eliot's claim that genuine poetry can communicate without being understood.

This emphasis on the *sound* of meaningful utterance is, of course, inseparable from its arising from the pleasure in the earliest playing between adult and infants, maybe a little older than Cannelle, but still very small, for example, "Pat-a-cake", when the baby has just learned to clap hands, whether only in imitation of the adult or, possibly, understanding some words and actions:

> Pat-a-cake, pat-a-cake, baker's man.
> Bake me a cake as fast as you can
> Pat it and prick it and mark it with B
> And put it in the oven for baby and me.

Here, prior to advanced verbal understanding, is a prime example of the instinctive making and "baking" of meaning *together*, usually initiated by the adult, with mental and physical activity involving all the senses. The activity also reinforces a baby's dawning awareness of difference and sameness.

Finally, such activity illustrates the simple relief and satisfaction for the child—and the psychotherapy patient—of hearing the sound of oneself, one's own voice speaking, one's own hands clapping, in the presence of a listening, participating other. In this game the baby is already involved in self-representation and performance.

CHAPTER THREE

A time and a place for playing: transitional phenomena

The activity of mirroring as a metaphor for holding, hearing, and full m/other–baby interaction sets the scene for Winnicott's transitional stage. This is an intermediate state where the infant, although, in Freud's words, still "his Majesty the baby" is beginning to recognize reality. Instead of being the centre of the world in oneness with the m/other, the baby begins to see the m/other as a separate person "out there". The gradually widening space between them furnishes a time and a place for playing, a time and place for the m/other also to become an imagined figure within the baby's own mind.

Linking the loss of the infant's primal illusions and the gain of symbolic power with playing between m/other and child softens this process of the *baby's* "inability and his growing ability to recognise and accept reality" (Winnicott, 1971, p. 3). For the Winnicott child, it is through playing: with the m/other, with objects, and alone, that the baby progresses. This playing becomes linked to all later forms of meaning-making, of playing in art and culture. In contrast with Freudian and Kleinian theories of the origins of art and culture as defensive against anxiety, playing and symbolic development are equated by Winnicott with creativity and aliveness.

Playing, the capacity for symbolic activity and adaptation to reality in Winnicott's account, centres partly on playing with an especially singled-out toy or teddy bear. This transitional object comes between the mother and baby. Like the breast itself, though provided by the m/other, the baby enjoys the illusion of having itself created this favoured possession:

> Winnicott's transitional object is half-way between the symbol and symbolic equation. The child's soft cuddly teddy or silky blanket reminds him of, stands for his mother's warmth and protectiveness and so helps him to go to sleep, as though she were still with him. In the transitional object stage, the child half knows the teddy bear is really only a substitute for the mother, and half denies this, telling himself that teddy is all it needs. [Alvarez, 1992, p. 44]

And, as importantly stressed in the following, it is, from the outset, words and speech that are the conduit for this process, which includes the further achievement of becoming a "bad enough child":

> Winnicott's "potential space", elaborated by a transitional object perfects the necessary conditions for semiotic functioning and transition to language acquisition . . . the potential space is a space from which to challenge the parents' language, to be, one might say, a "bad enough child". [Wright, 1984, p. 99]

For Winnicott, it is as much the early relationship to the infant's *teddy bear* as original possession of the *mother's body* that inspires creative activity with materials in the outside world. Immersion in drama or a theatrical performance, playing with paint, plasticine, sand, or musical sound, revives the transitional state of both creating something that is not self and experiencing a sensual satisfaction akin to the original mother–infant–teddy bear relationship of the transitional stage. It is to the relationship with the transitional object that, in Winnicott's thinking, we can trace the source of the transforming properties of imagination. For with the transitional object there appears the first freeing of the imagination by means of a symbol and the first experiences of imaginative interaction. It sometimes looks as if the father in Winnicott's theatre plays second fiddle to the teddy bear.

What matters, as well as its symbolic significance, is that this blanket or teddy bear exists as an actual object in the world. When the child begins to use some thing as a stand-in for the mother, this widens the space between them. This furthers the possibility of sequence, duration, essential to early symbolic activity—meaning-making, the sustaining of an image, the linking of two or more thoughts. In this way, the child's playing and its relationship to transitional objects is seen as the prototype of playing in music, theatre, plays, and other rituals, where, as in psychotherapy, setting and duration are key components. The much used teddy bear becomes the derivative of whatever materials constitute a particular art form—words, music, paint, performance, etc.

From the child's relationship to such objects comes the dawning perception that one thing can *stand for* another, *as if* it were that other, which is a step towards mastery of similarities, differences, and the making of meaning. And in the midst of artistic or cultural activity of all kinds, in theatre and in therapy, it is the shaky status of this *as if* factor that is the hallmark of the transitional. In the relationship between inner and outer, between illusion and reality, and, supremely, between me and not me, *as if* is always in danger of slipping into "the same as", the symbol or sign or word becoming more real than its referent. Here, where illusion might become equated with reality is the particular source and province of all forms of playing and creativity—and also of madness:

> In staking a claim for an intermediate state between a baby's inability and his growing ability to recognise and accept reality, I am therefore studying the substance of ILLUSION, that which is allowed to the infant, and which in adult life is inherent in religion and art, and yet becomes a hallmark of madness when an adult puts too powerful a claim on the credulity of others, forcing them to share an illusion that is not their own. [Winnicott, 1971, p. 3]

Because communication between mother and infant occurs from the beginning, and because, in the earliest phase, it is possible that the infant has no idea that this mother *is* other, it gets used to what it mistakes for perpetual *self* communication, communication with a presumed part of oneself. If this view is correct, this transitional stage, with the beginnings of separation from m/other, must include some sense of loss of *self*, as well as loss of m/other. So the teddy bear helps to compensate for this seeming loss of "me", as mother becomes "you" or "other". The bear comes to represent not only the mother, but also the "me" "out there". It becomes the first of the numberless others infused by the self in all areas of experience. This need to have part of oneself *outside* is a major impetus for the conferring of imaginative life and qualities on the object, and of supplying it with the function of a communicating alter ego, which the infant once took for granted in the form of the m/other (cf. Richards, 2002, pp. 194–195).

The cotton reel game

The early relationship with a created transitional object is a prelude to the action captured in Freud's account of his baby grandson, in what became known as the "Fort Da" game (Freud, 1908, p. 213). This example centres on the crucial accompaniment of spoken words. By means of the threaded cotton reel that the baby was repeatedly hurling away from his cot and hauling back, crying "gone!" and "here!", he was showing his mastery of continuity: the absent mother would return, for he could now imagine her in her not-there-ness. He knew the cotton reel was not his mother, but her absence—the space between them—helped to tickle his imagination and propel him into the symbolic, into speech. The child had "absolutely no need of a nursery full of toys. *He could contrive to convey his meaning with anything at all*" (Mannoni, 1987, p. 19). This child was indeed no longer infans (non-speaking). In savouring the power and satisfaction of words, he found that "how pleasant it is to act through the hands of others and to move the world simply by moving the tongue" (Rousseau, 1997, p. 10) and inhabit an inner world of imagination.

Thus, the "Fort Da" game points, in turn, towards that later mixture of illusion and reality in the toddler's tea party, where not only will "*anything at all*" *do*, but words and gestures alone suffice. For the toddlers, in pouring out and handing round their *invisible* cups of tea to their real or imaginary companions, are now aware that illusion and reality are intermingled. Already, the small child's imagination is able to be fully caught up in the playing, while simultaneously knowing that this is only pretending. Such pure creative playing, dependent on no-thing at all, not even the teddy bear, is a further step in symbolic imaginative activity: through words, musical composition, choreography, visual art, etc.

In later childhood and adolescence, and perhaps forever, there is a fascinating further twist to this process, when, even in the very presence of the object/other, the *sign* of that other's presence may be of higher importance. For presence alone can never make up for the inborn lack that is the price of being human and for the fact that, as noted by Nietzsche, "the word is the murderer of the thing". This is illustrated in the following account by Rousseau of his feelings for his guardian, Madame de Warens—"Maman":

> I would never finish if I were to describe in detail all the follies that the recollection of my dear Maman made me commit when I was no longer in her presence. How often I kissed my bed, recalling that she had slept in it, my curtains and all the furniture in the room, since they belonged to her and her beautiful hand had touched them, even the floor, on which I prostrated myself, thinking that she had walked on it. [Culler, 1983, p. 11]

Then, still more bizarrely, he continues,

> But sometimes even in her presence I committed extravagances that only the most violent love seemed capable of inspiring. One day at table, just as she had put a piece of food in her mouth, I exclaimed that I saw a hair on it. She put the morsel back on her plate; I eagerly seized and swallowed it. [*ibid.*]

Bearness and thereness

However, Winnicott's insistence that the transitional object's "not being the breast (or the mother), although real, is as important as the fact that it stands for the mother", (Winnicott, 1971, p. 6) makes a vital contribution also to the dimension of *"non-meaning"* as an inescapable and necessary part of living.

To concede the existence of the bear for its own sake conceptualizes not only the child's adaptation to external reality and meaning-making, but it also allows for a possible, even necessary pull *against*

the symbolic, against meaning-making: a bear is a bear is a bear
. . . As well as the bear's symbolic functions, that bear also counts
and matters in its "thereness" or "bearness". There is value in its
very concreteness and singularity, because the process of meaning-
making requires a space for the possibility of non-meaning.

The very "thisness" of the precious teddy bear looms up to
obstruct this universal drive towards standing back and insisting
that "reality"—life—possesses meaning beyond the immediate and
given. The bearness and thereness invite immersion in the immediate *for its own sake*; one might say, in the best interests of truth.
For the power and need to make sense of the world and one's
experience, to use symbols, to form patterns, which render reality
palatable, implies also the potential opposite of these things:
the need and the right *not* to make meaning, the appropriate acceptance of non-meaning, which I think is not to be confused with
meaninglessness.

A dimension of non-meaning confers equality of status on the
manifest, the surface, the concrete, regardless of the deeper or the
hidden. Allowing for the presence of randomness, acceptance of
possible non-meaning checks and subverts that irresistible urge for
satisfying explanations of the inexplicable, which is a remnant of
our primal omnipotence: as insisted by Job, "There must be a *reason*
for all my misfortunes".

In public as in private life, the drive for reasons, explanations,
justifications proves irresistible and excessive. An especially striking manifestation of this is illustrated in a (long-ago) *Guardian* article, referring to the "Just World Syndrome". This is the primitive
assumption that the victim must have deserved his/her punish-
ment. In a case of alleged rape by a total stranger, in his summing
up the judge took into account that the victim had been wearing a
mini-skirt when she was attacked. It was reasoned that the woman
had therefore partly "caused" the rape. The mini-skirt "made more
sense" of the rapist's behaviour, somehow mitigating, if not the
victim's, then everyone else's distress.

In psychotherapy, too, the concept of non-meaning in counter-
point with meaning liberates patient and analyst to accept, when
appropriate, an absence of connecting links, or of interpretation and
explanations. The counterpointing of meaning-making with non-
meaning that characterizes transitional states is replicated in

psychotherapy in its blend of illusion and reality. The framed-off space and the pressure of a strictly controlled time recreate the conditions experienced by the tot with its teddy bear, and by the two-year-old playing at tea parties. It involves the power to maintain a tension between illusion and reality, and so play in Winnicott's intermediate, transitional space.

The context of the following extract is Renée's convalescence on a farm to which Sechehaye had been sending top quality apples from town:

I was led to modify the psychoanalytic treatment in order to reach the patient's emotions, and help her out of the walled enclosure of her unreality. The simplest means of contact which I used was *to realise the unconscious desire, according to the symbolism presented by the patient*. I would like to stress already now that the symbols were reality to the patient — in fact, the only reality they were symbols merely for the analyst.

Renée runs away from the farm where she was convalescing, and arrives at my house all alone at night, in terrible agony. I persist in trying to understand the symbolism of the apples. To the remark that I had given her as many little apples as she wanted, Renée cries "Yes, but those are store apples, apples for big people, but I want apples from Mummy, like that, pointing to my breasts. Those apples there, Mummy gives them only when one is hungry." I understand at last what must be done. Since the apples represent maternal milk, I must give them to her Renée directly, feeding her baby. I must give her the symbol myself, directly and without intermediary, and at a fixed hour. To verify my hypothesis I carry it out at once. Taking an apple and cutting it in two I offer Renée a piece, saying "It is to drink the milk from Mummy's apples, Mummy is going to give it to you." Renée then leans up against my shoulder, presses the apple on my breast, and very solemnly, with intense happiness, eats it.

The symbolism of the apples was the removal of all the shocks that Renée had had in infancy in regard to food, which represents maternal love. First of all, the mother had put so much water in the milk that it had hardly had any consistency at all, and I could not satisfy the child. [Sechehaye 1951, p. 44]

What is revealed here with such clarity is how "the symbols were reality to the patient — in fact, the only reality." Without this evidence, one might have expected Renée to refer to Mother Sechehaye's apple as the "milk" it actually represented for her. Instead, she insists on "apples from Mummy, like that", pointing to my breasts. "Those apples there, Mummy gives them only when one is hungry".

CHAPTER FOUR

"An act apart": meaning-making in theatre and therapy

"The arena, the card-table, the magic circle, the temple, the stage, the screen, the tennis-court, the court of justice, etc. are all in form and function play-grounds—that is, forbidden spots, isolated, hedged round, hallowed, within which special rules obtain . . . All are temporary worlds within the ordinary world dedicated to the performance of an act apart"

(Huizinga, 1949: p. 10, quoted in Farhi, 1991)

"No human being is free from relating inner and outer reality, and relief from this strain is provided by an intermediate area of experience which is not challenged"

(Winnicott, 1971 , p. 13)

Theatre

The themes of meaning-making, playing, in an intermediate space/time between m/other and baby introduce the parallels between being in psychotherapy and being in the theatre. The compression of all the world to a stage or an empty space for playing in both the theatre and the setting of psychotherapy lays bare the normally less perceptible phenomena of time, space, and meaning-making.

In the celebrated System of the great Russian stage theorist, Stanislavsky (Stanislavsky, 1936), certain insights and images for actors appear as precursors of emerging psychoanalytic ideas. Stanislavsky's whole approach is based on awareness of the power of the unconscious, (which he refers to as the "sub-conscious") "in motivating behaviour". The "set of rules", the convention, between the two parties involved—audience and actors, therapist and patient—which establishes a necessary, but not necessarily understood, boundary between them, is described by Stanislavsky as the invisible "fourth wall" of the proscenium arch. As for the concept and nature of the invisible "wall" in theatre-in-the-round, there is a still more powerful tension in the greater proximity between actors and audience.

According to Stanislavsky, this invisible fourth wall both protects the actor from the terrifying "black hole" of the auditorium and also aids the achievement of "communion" with the other actors and "re-fusion" with the audience, who, with the actors, are caught up in the power of what Stanislavsky calls the "magic if", which I see as identical to the "as if" of the analytic situation: the "magic if brings to life what is hidden behind the words".

Stanislavsky states further that "in the audience the actor sees a 'mirror of his performance'", assigning to the audience a perhaps more passive role than may be applicable to the highly dynamic reactions, both internal and external, of such a group. In this portrayal of the spectator's near-regressive state, there is an echo of images already introduced here, in Chapter Two, associated with the m/other–infant relationship and that apply to the situation of psychotherapy.

Facilitated by these special conditions, the womb-like darkness of the auditorium for the spectators and the security of the consulting room for the patient, meaning-making and projections on to the actors/therapist are magnified. There is a regressive pull towards merging and away from separateness. In this space, illusion may now contend equally with reality.

For it is primarily this invisible partition that permits the creation or opening up of that space or "temporary world within the ordinary world" (above) for the advent of the "magic if" of theatre and the "as if" of therapy—a negotiated and willing suspension of disbelief. The activity around the boundary, the "fourth wall", which defines this space is a key factor in activating the intensified emotional activity and the play of meaning-making between the participants.

As demonstrated in semiotic theory—the theory of signs—in any human system, organization or "code" nothing can be excluded from this activity of meaning-making or interpretation. It is not possible not to infer meaning, whether consciously or unconsciously. It is equally not possible for oneself to be protected from the meaning-making of others.

The obvious example of dress and style illustrates this. For, no matter what attire you choose, including sheer nudity, it will not be possible to prevent observers projecting on to, as well as taking in, messages and information from what you are wearing, including make-up or its absence. Yet whatever meanings are inferred or conferred will be largely shaped by the conventions of your particular culture and society, the particular context and, above all, by its interrelations with all the other elements in the structure and setting.

This applies still more when a particular setting is cordoned off and ordinary social conventions are repealed. Then this meaning-making process is so intensified that it can be borne away by its own momentum. For, as the theatre semiotician Keir Elam said, "All that is on the stage is a sign" (Elam, 1980, p. 7). "All" refers to all the theatrical "codes" involved in a performance. These include not only the paramount codes of speech and action, but such props as lighting, costume, make-up, stage set, gesture, facial expression, body language, and spatial relationships. Nor is any one of these absent from the stage of psychotherapy.

If all that is on the stage is a sign, nothing is simply itself; everything is at one remove; everything is a representation, but far more so than in the outside world. And paradoxically, the generation of illusion on the stage and in the texts of plays owes less to naturalistic presentation than to the interpretative attitude of the spectator or reader. Here is habitation of Winnicott's transitional or "third" area, where illusion and reality, self and other, intermingle.

However instantly, for example, we may recognize and identify on the stage a naturalistic-looking tree because of its framing-off on the stage, this tree can be said also to *represent* a tree. And the spectator would also experience as an equally valid representation of a tree either a one-dimensional painting or even a stick planted in the ground with a placard pinned there designating "tree". Further, *live* animals that appear in theatrical performances could similarly, be said to be *representing* these animals.

In Chekhov's *The Seagull*, the young writer Constantin stages a play within the *Seagull* play. Constantin's play is supposed to take place outdoors in the evening. Constantin insists on the performance being timed for the exact appearance of the "real" moon in the "real" sky. It can therefore be said that, while within the "real" world of *The Seagull*, the reality of that world's moon is provided by some form of stage lighting, in the fictional play by Chekhov's invented character, Constantin, this illusory/real moon is itself turned into a stage prop as part of the intended secondary dramatic illusion. Thus, simultaneously, we have the staged moon lit by lighting designers of *The Seagull*, which, for the characters, is a real moon. But for the cast playing the people created by the character Constantin, their "real" moon becomes again a stage prop. So the moon of the *The Seagull*'s live audience has more in common with the moon of Constantin's at-one-remove, play-within-the-play figures than with the moon of Chekhov's primary set of characters.

Thus, illusion and the "as if" effect can function on more than one level and is generated largely by collaborative acts between the participants. For whatever appears before the audience tends to be accepted unconditionally and simultaneously as both real and not real within the particular established convention and aided by the transforming agency of the imagination. As with the original infant and its teddy bear, the imagination is ever ready to recreate, interpret, and appropriate for itself the data of experience, to inhabit the domain of illusion and reality.

This impulse to impute meaning is further illustrated by the case of an actress whose role required her to be bare-legged on stage, and who, during the interval of one performance got a bad scratch on her leg. Appearing with this vivid sign after the interval, the spectators then speculated with great animation on the significance of this new scratch, which was automatically assumed to be a deliberate representation and a part of the performance. In the outside world, though, while we might question how someone got a bad scratch, its possible meaning would hardly occupy us with such intensity.

No matter how stylized a presentation may be, as in the work of Bertolt Brecht, the dissident counterpart of Stanislavsky, this signifying activity by the spectator/patient, in both theatre and therapy, is charged with an intensified emotional response. Brecht sought to encourage the spectators' critical detachment and to prevent their regressive impulse to be caught up in an imaginary world, divorced from harsh reality. In contrast to Stanislavsky, Brecht kept the house lights on throughout a performance and employed other distancing methods. Yet his devices failed to prevent his audiences from being transported and identified with the stage-world.

For audiences were no less moved by the mask that coexisted alongside the actor and revealed him than by the mask that hid the actor. This point is illustrated by the following anecdote concerning the staging of Brecht's play *On Consent*, in which his purpose was to convey a truth without involving the spectator's over-identification with stage figures:

> In order to demonstrate how inhuman people are to one another, Brecht constructed a clown figure with monstrously extended wooden legs and arms and a very large, very obviously false head. The patently false extremities of the first clown were then sawn off in a way which exaggerated the act of sawing. Despite the patently non-naturalistic character of the clown figure, it is reported that the grotesque sawing of the clown's wooden limbs and head caused members of the audience to faint because of the gruesomeness of the scene. [Fuesil, 1981]

A particularly fruitful exploitation of this borderline relationship between spectators and actors occurs at the very end of Samuel Beckett's brief masterpiece *Catastrophe*, where a fascist theatre director issues commands to his assistant concerning the "arrangement" of a human figure on the stage for an imaginary audience, but also, of course, for us, the real audience. This male figure is totally reified, treated solely as a stage prop, rendered null and impotent. Just before the end, however the assistant suggests that the figure should be made to raise his head a little. This is scornfully refused by the director, who issues a final lighting command: "Stop! Now let them have it!"

Beckett's stage directions now specify: [*Fade out of general light. Pause. Fade out of light on body. Light on* bowed *head alone. Long pause.*] Then the Director comments, "Terrific. He'll have them on their feet. I can hear it from here." Beckett's stage directions continue: [*Pause. Distant sound of recorded applause.*] i.e. from the *imaginary* audience.

Then the human figure, in defiance of the imposed *bowed* position entirely on his own initiative, actually does raise his head and fixes his gaze on the audience, i.e. the *real* theatre audience (ourselves), thus performing an autonomous act. But—and here is the equivocal nature of our relationship between illusion and reality under these conditions—the stage directions now instruct: [*The recorded applause now falters, dies. There is a long pause followed by fadeout of light on face.*] And this is the finale of the play, which, according to convention, is the signal for *us*, the real audience, to applaud. But what are we now applauding? For the timing implies that not only are we clapping Beckett's play, but that willy-nilly, we are collaborating with that last action: the fade-out of the man's raised head. For Beckett has delegated the lighting to the fascist Director, who thus crushes the figure's gesture of freedom. So, by adroitly exploiting the tension between the real and the not real, facilitated by the "fourth wall" or proscenium arch, Beckett effectively challenges and unsettles the position of the real audience, introducing a confusion between representation and actuality.

Therapy as theatre

And in psychotherapy, contending with the inflation of meaning-making and fantasy, there is the urge to accept as "natural" whatever constitutes the ritual, through repetition and through all the features of the setting.

Whether the therapist opens the door to the patient or uses an entryphone; whether s/he speaks or is silent at the end of a session; whether s/he regularly shakes hands on arrival or departure, or never shakes hands; whether the use of the couch is optional or obligatory, all this, in combination with the "props"—the established objects and furnishings of the room, the habitual sounds, the therapist's costume, their relative physical position in the allotted space—become as much part of the total setting and expected order as the timing of sessions, the regularity, and the payment of fees. Everything is both apparently "natural", inevitable, and loaded with meaning. All these elements are the supporting cast of speech, with gesture and body language, perhaps more equal than supporting.

Yet if there then occurs any alteration in the setting or ritual, if the relationship between the elements is disturbed, this results in a fresh explosion of meaning. The patient can no more help ascribing powerful reasons and motives for any chance deviation than could the audience reacting to the scratch on the actor's leg.

If, for example, when the buzzer sounds the door refuses to open because the therapist has forgotten to draw back the bolt, or is late home from some—inexcusable—trip, if there is a new picture on the wall, if something is missing in the room, if the therapist fails to shake hands, or, suddenly, for the first time, were to shake hands; if a member of the therapist's family bursts into the room, not realizing a session is in progress—any such deviations can be world-shaking and charged with heightened significance. As in the theatre, so the "infinite riches in the little room" (Marlowe's *Jew of Malta*) of therapy, arouse senses, thoughts, and feelings to fever pitch.

The "tape-recording"

A patient in a long and sometimes stormy analysis, reacted strongly to signs of sleepiness in the normally attentive therapist after an Easter break. The patient had been relating matters of vital moment and, although she had directly voiced her frustration and feelings of paralysis, her anger persisted into the next session when, to her surprise, the therapist showed himself to have complete recall of yesterday's material, despite his apparent inattentiveness. As the patient descended the stairs after the session, she heard what sounded like a click, which she realized always sounded as she came and went. She became instantly convinced that her sessions were tape-recorded, irrationally assuming that what the therapist couldn't listen to live, he could—and would—nevertheless bone up on later. After a sleepless night spent fuming at the therapist's perfidy, a tiny chink appeared in the patient's certainty and by the time she reached her session, conviction had now shrunk to fantasy, which she disclosed to the therapist. The latter for once dropped his analytic stance, expressing himself baffled about the "click" and inviting the patient to alert him the next time it occurred. Instead of the sinister switch of a tape recorder, it proved to be the smoke alarm and the patient's suspicions subsided.

The patient's shakiness and vulnerability cause her mistrust to rise up in reaction to the analyst's unsatisfactory, sleepy response. This tangle of actions and reactions, projections and introjections, result in the paranoid foregrounding of a single innocuous element in the total setting: the misrecognized sound of a smoke alarm. "Everything on the stage" is indeed "a sign" and the overloading of one signifier exposes the thinness of the "as if" line, which on this occasion had to be breached by the therapist as well as the patient (Richards, 2002, pp. 198–199).

CHAPTER FIVE

Analytic interpretation: games and playing

F or Winnicott, playing is associated with spontaneity, aliveness, creativity. The capacity to play implies a fullness of being, spaciousness, and presentness. Playing is open-ended, with world and time enough. In creative playing, it is the process that counts, whereas in what I am loosely designating "games", outcome is more important. The focus is on winning. Both are potentially exciting, precarious, and aggressive—the chess board may be overturned in rage at the height of a game, the football match may break up in an unseemly scuffle. And as my final material in Chapter Eighteen indicates, games can act as a necessary stepping-stone towards creative playing.

People feel held or contained by the time limit involved in many organized games. From the beginning the end is in sight, and this time factor supplies additional structure to disturbed and fragmented people. Because games are more closed and proceed more by external, fixed rules, they depend on primarily cognitive processes and conscious thinking. These are qualities no less essential to psychological health than open-ended playing and free association. Games possess the security of explicit aims and are more concerned with control and knowing—or trying to know—in advance, though there is, of course, an overlap: playing need be no less aggressive than games. But, as observed by the writer Zbigniew Kotowicz, "The space of play is not teleological" (Kotowicz, 1997, p. 145).

An implicit distinction between games and playing is encapsulated by the scene in *Great Expectations* when Miss Havisham infamously commands the young Pip at his first visit: "Play, boy, play!" In this meeting, playing has neither a time nor a place. The potentially shared space between child and adult is wholly filled by the self-obsessed Miss Havisham. Instead of mirroring Pip, she communes with and comments on her *own* reflection in the looking-glass. Time in Miss Havisham's domain is concretely frozen at a single moment in the past, which strangles the vital present. Upon the impossible command, "Play, boy, play!" Pip contemplates, but then dismisses, a *simulation* of playing, with "the desperate idea of starting round the room in the assumed character of Mr Pumble-chook's chaise-cart". But a free imaginative act of spontaneously "being" or representing Mr Pumblechook is blocked by Pip's panic. The situation is finally resolved in an antithesis of free playing, when Miss Havisham orders Pip to partake in a *game* of cards with the disdainful Estella.

In psychotherapy, whether an encounter between therapist and patient falls more into these loose categories of games or of playing, or, indeed, of "toying" or "trifling", is inseparable from that therapist's imagined position and what he or she does with his or her analytic "understanding" of the patient. All hinges on a fine-tuning of the transference relationship. The therapist must judge and intuit the shifting needs of the patient. Is the focus primarily on the past and the patient's outside life, inviting explicit links between these and the figure of therapist? Is there an explicit, even exclusive focus on "inside", on what is happening *between* therapist and patient "here and now"? Or is the person of the therapist needed more as an unobtrusive someone, almost behind the scenes, enabling the action and the patient's inner musings to unfold?

While in practice we can expect an intermingling of these modalities and considerations, in what follows I review each as as a separate strand in the whole pattern, devoting Chapter Seven to the function of the unobtrusive analyst.

Back to the past

A recursive transference approach carries an assumption, some-times in rather a concrete way, that the patient projects on to the therapist key figures and behaviour from his or her own life. Applied too diligently, this can appear mechanical and simplistic, almost rule-driven, insisting that the therapist is supposed always to be representing someone else for the patient. The complex patterns of response, the intricacy and richness of the connection with the living, present person of the therapist, are then suppressed, cheapened, and reified.

For the therapist's own distinctive personality may elicit from the patient never-before-experienced reactions and behaviour: a brand new structure of thought and feeling might be emerging that, whatever its roots in the past, belongs more to the present and future. Yet in a therapist's "Back to the past" mode, there is a tendency to treat passionate expressions by the patient of both posi-tive and negative feelings towards the therapist by immediately transposing such feelings to other figures or events in the patient's life, whether dear, dead, or near. The patient feels cheated, sold short. The room grows dark, as s/he suspects that the therapist is dodging the challenge of the lived reality between them. When this transference device becomes predictable, as if it is in obedience to a prescribed rule, the experience conforms more closely to games than to playing. As described by the Lacanian analyst, Leavy:

> To be told, however convincingly, that one does so and so because one loved one's sister at a certain time in childhood, as clearly manifested by a specific memory, is not the same as to utter, to speak, maybe to shout, in affect-laden words, right now, that long withheld desire. [Leavy, 1983, p. 15]

Here and now

In an emphasis on the here-and-now transference, the patient's material and whatever happens in a session, all the elements in the setting, are treated in terms of the immediate therapist–patient rela-tionship. This mode furnishes the therapist with an instrument of amazing, if sometimes questionable, power.

Here, the therapist does not necessarily make explicit connections with other times, places, and people. What the participants are "Doing to [and with] Each Other: (Hubback, 1988) here and now is felt to suffice as an unconscious manifestation of the past, subsumed in the present of the analytic relationship—a bird in the hand is worth two in the past.

From his/her transference communications, seen as directed to the person/figure of the therapist and extended to the whole of the analytic setting, the patient is encouraged to experience and express increasingly elemental, primitive passions and needs. This might be seen as helping the patient to connect with the "child within" or the "true self", perhaps bringing a revival of infancy feelings. With increasing dependence on the therapist comes a blurring of boundaries and a longing for oneness. Such dependent states are reflected in an intriguing semantic deviation.

This is an apparent dissolution of linguistic opposites. In response to the patient's yearnings, the therapist's manner is correspondingly affected, consciously or otherwise. In possibly involuntary, soothing tones, s/he might say, for example, "You are telling me that you want to be close to me", or "You are sad that you must leave me". And it can be as if the patient directly hears the longed-for equivalent of the analyst's declaring the opposite, "*I* want to be close to *you*", and "*I* am sad that *you* must leave me". Here, there is immense emotional and often erotic impact. If the patient laments the analyst's impending break and the analyst, says tenderly, "You are afraid that I want to get rid of you", the patient, in this state, is quite likely to fall gratefully on the therapist's words—or her tone—as meaning, "Of course I *don't* want to get rid of you". The open-endedness of the actual analytic statement may be quite lost on the patient.

The strangeness of such semantic reversals and their aural impact in both analytic and literary experience, were remarked by Freud in relation to dream work "where contraries are treated in the same way as conformities". He points out that a "welcome analogy to this strange behaviour is provided for us in the development of language, where contraries such as 'light–dark', 'strong–weak', 'big–small' are said by some philologists to be expressed by the same verbal root" (Bowie, in Sturrock, 1982, p. 214).

Thus the blurring of difference in certain psychic states, in the drive towards oneness, primary unity, with the m/other/therapist, is accompanied by a reversion to more primitive ways of thought. The switch of pronouns in the *patient's* interpretation of the *therapist's* interpretation bring about an emotional relief similar to the sensation of satisfied thirst.

For the main efficacy of here and now transference interpretations lies in the paradox that the articulation or reflecting back of the patient's lack, longing and other extreme emotions, generates its own solace. This response is what Bollas calls "the effects of the analyst's song", which he regards as sometimes even more potent than the meaning of h/er words.

But, as expressed by the analyst, Michael Balint, who, like Winnicott, is associated with the Independent school of psychoanalysis, such music is seen as not entirely wholesome:

> Words lose their reliability as agreed means of communication between patient and analyst; interpretations, in particular, tend to be experienced by the patient either as signs of hostility and aggressiveness, or of affection. The patient begins to know too much about the analyst; it is a fairly common occurrence that he is more aware of his analyst's moods than of his own; parallel with this, his interest apparently becomes more and more detached from his own problems and sufferings, which originally prompted him to seek analytic help, and gets centred more and more on divining the analyst's "real motives" for saying this, for behaving in that way, or for having a particular "mood". [Balint, 1959, p. 231]

Balint's commentary is further revealing in its lack of any reference to the analyst's own possible contribution to such behaviour in his patient. Yet in such regressed states, the therapist surely plays a part not restricted solely to vocal modulations. Whether in order to foster the patient's state or in response to it, not only are the tone and manner of the therapist bound to be modified by the patient's appeal, but also his or her own language tends to become "dumbed down". Subtleties, degrees and shades of meaning, give way to such infant extremes as, for example, "good", "bad", "angry", "nice", "nasty", "naughty". Nuances of advanced vocabulary, in all their richness of association, may then turn into *1984*'s nightmarish outlawing of concepts and, hence, of feelings, reducing the entire original articulated spectrum of feeling to "good–ungood".

So, while those patients for whom this austere diet of transference interpretation is like nectar feel wondrously known, held, and fed by the analyst, others who are fragile or without a strong network of support find that the gaps between sessions, the feelings of lack, hunger, and longing aroused by interpretations delivered more from "above" than "alongside" are sometimes almost unbearable.

There is a contradiction in the therapist's apparent fostering of such strong dependence while s/he is actually here and then switching the patient off at the end of sessions and, notoriously, before breaks, even refusing to disclose any idea of his/her where-abouts. This elevates the symbolic/fantasy aspect of the relation-ship to the exclusion of the real human relationship. It is when the analyst underestimates the extent of a patient's dependence and difficulty in managing the gaps between meetings that the work ceases to be playing and seems to turn into games, in a cat-and-mouse fashion. Whether from a failure to grasp the measure of the patient's condition, or from a certain sadistic pleasure; whether from disaffection, or from being excessively wedded to a chosen technique, or for her own self-protection, the therapist appears to be toying or trifling, rather than playing, with the patient.

These pangs of the patient, who is offered no spot in the whole world where s/he may rest his/her gaze during the separation is sometimes deemed beneficial to the patient's progress. Yet I know of no evidence for this. On the contrary, the indications are that cavalier treatment can interminably perpetuate the therapy, keeping alive the patient's hope that *one day* the therapist will unequivocally want him/her . . .

For even when, over years of therapy, transference interpreta-tions have inevitably dwindled, it is possible that the patient will remain captive to their original power, to the thrills of that austere regime. Understood by some writers as "malign regression" (Balint, 1968, p. 119ff). this protracted adhesion to the person of the analyst and the magic of his/her words and presence, delays the integra-tion of thought and feeling that is one purpose of transference inter-pretation.

To some extent, this issue revolves around the distinction made by the Independent school of analysts between "needs" on the one hand and "wishes" or "desire" on the other. Needs are seen as legit-imate and potentially able to be met, because they are in a sense primitive and implicitly "innocent", even non-sexual, while wishes or desire are more sexually tinged, associated with demands for indulgence and therefore should not be gratified. But such a distinction surely dissolves in the following spin on desire by Lacan: "Man's desire finds its meaning in the desire of the other, not so much because the other holds the key to the object desired, as because the first object of desire is to be recognised by the other" (Lacan, 1954, p. 235).

Stanislavsky concludes, "A character-emotion is the mask which hides the actor individual. Protected by it, he can lay bare his soul to the last intimate detail" (Stanislavsky, 1958, p. 30).

According to this conception, only by use of the mask covering the face can the actor's soul truly serve the character he is playing. The mask's full reality, born of illusion, bears a meaning that, while mediated by the "soul" of the actor, is nevertheless identical with it. (Although "soul" is unfashionable and so must be distinguished from the "self" with connotations of immortality, in Stanislavsky's usage "soul" appears synonymous with the idea of one's whole being informing an activity. "Personality" is perhaps the closest contemporary word. But after all, "soul" is the direct translation of "psyche," and "soul" is more careful than "self" in analytic work, as depicted in both Freud's Soul and plays.) Such is the nature of the Stanislavsky mask of the actor expressing life, its rendering of truth through illusion and revelation through concealment, with no implication of falseness.

George Devine, the former director of the Royal Court Theatre, in his experimental work with masks laid bare a truth expressing the desire to be one less burdened, the Mask. It was quite common in that the wearer therein beheld not at the sight of the Mask was the that is the release. The actor's entire personality was subdued as the character of that Mask; the initial is capitalized because by then a would address not the actor but only the Mask, as did the actor when in pretend. The actors were sometimes unable to shed their Mask character even at the end of an improvisation session and fell into its hold.

So has the actor, protected by the mask of his/her character, the actor really lay bare his soul to the last intimate detail? A caution is placed particularly when free masks become "forced", when that same mask over one's own role can leave the actor scarred and marked by its personality and pathology. The distinction between the "uncontrolled" self and its masks is then lost. For example, an actor playing the evil old man in Strindberg's Ghost Sonata would "leave the theatre every night with my knees knocking, in a most disturbing" (1971, p. 39). It is also well known that several years ago said Day Lewis, playing Hamlet, that from the National Theatre stage convinced that Hamlet's father's ghost was an apparition of his own father — Day Lewis. In both of these cases it seemed as if initially free masks turned into forced masks.

CHAPTER SIX

Interpretation and playing: freedom of association

The unobtrusive analyst

"Analytical" understanding of our patients *can* have a *wholesomely* destructive effect, like a cauterization, but on sound tissue it is *damagingly* destructive . . . it is a technique we have learned from the devil . . . the threatening and dangerous thing about analysis is that the individual is apparently *understood*: the devil eats away the soul which, naked and exposed, robbed of its protective shell, was born like a child into the light. [Jung, 1915, p. 199, italics added]

This attack on what Jung refers to "analytical understanding" refers, I think, to a position where the analyst appears to "know"; whose stance is experienced as too much above and too little beside the patient. In what appears to be a celebration of the trusting nakedness that arises from a non-penetrative analytic experience, "understanding" is seen as devouring, probing, corrosive, even raping. It carries the suggestion that, for an insecure patient, such "understanding" breaches an already fragile divide, with the therapist installing him or herself, uninvited, at the very heart of the patient's being. Like Hamlet, reacting to Rosencrantz's and Guildernstern's probing, the patient may feel the therapist seeks to "pluck out the heart of my mystery". Yet, as reflected by Winnicott, if it is "a joy to be hidden", it is also "a disaster not be found". To hold on to both sides of the paradox, another kind of understanding must be brought into play, which takes into account the patient's immediate emotional state.

Beth's Law: "Don't tell me what I feel"

In the case of Beth, it took her therapist a long time to grasp exactly why she experienced certain interpretations as intrusive and destructive rather than creative, dropping rather than holding, until the following occasion.

Beth launched into an angry diatribe at the therapist's iniquities, leading him to respond with, "I think you feel that I have betrayed you". Beth grew still more incensed, declaring that she couldn't stand the therapist's "text book interpretations".

He wondered why his comment had seemed "text bookish" and Beth replied, "Well *I* didn't use the word 'betray'. It was *your* word." Then after a long pause, she added grudgingly that perhaps it *was* the right word. But it wasn't *her* word. So it felt very intrusive. When the therapist asked what might therefore have felt better, Beth's answer was, "It would have been OK if you had just asked, 'Do you feel betrayed?'"

Here, Beth thought she would prefer a direct question, which would not imply from the therapist a privileged understanding, barred to herself. A direct question would feel less piercing. Beth experienced the intervention as challenging her own desperately needed control—of the session, of the words, the thoughts, of the therapist, of time and space.

In his zeal to make meaning, to act as the bringer of light and understanding to the patient—"*you feel that I have betrayed you*"—the therapist missed out a necessary stage of the process, by failing first to register her fury and to attempt to explore this with her. She needed a real person, *alongside* her, wrestling with her meaning, not seemingly handing down his wisdom from on high. Demand for overt acknowledgement of what is happening between therapist and patient has to be suspended in favour of the therapist's acting rather as a facilitating presence. Otherwise, he is seen, however unfairly, to be pointing at himself, insisting on "me, me, me!"

Frances—"Don't foist your issues on me!"

Frances, sensitive and prickly to the point of paranoia, had elevated her therapist sky-high, trusting him sufficiently to undergo an intense, wholly unsolicited regressive experience. Then, after nearly a year's work, the therapy foundered on a single sequence.

Frances began the session by introducing her wish to take her break at a time when she knew the therapist would still be working. Despite this knowledge, she began by saying, in solicitous tones, that she knew how much the therapist would be needing a break and that he should take it when she had to take hers. Feeling somewhat manipulated, he replied that, as discussed earlier, he *would* still be working at that time. Frances digested this and then asked if he would expect her to pay for her missed sessions.

Instead of pondering this, the therapist, nettled by the patient's take-over bid, replied immediately that he probably *would* charge her something, but that they could discuss it further. She hastily and in some agitation replied, "No, no. There is no need. You have made your position clear. It is quite settled. It is fine . . ."

Frances then needed instantly to expel into the therapist and disown any dangerously negative sentiments of her own towards him, which threatened her idealization. So she strove to wrest back whatever available control was left to her. To the therapist's suggestion that Frances was very disappointed in his answer, she coldly denied it, repeating, "Certainly not. Of course I shall pay you . . . But what I *really* want to talk about is . . ." and she launched into a quite different topic, while the therapist was left feeling heavily rebuked by the blast of her polite anger.

So it seemed to him essential, when there was a pause in her ensuing "more pressing" topic, to revert to her possibly still angry feelings about payment during the break. This intervention was devastating to Frances. She denounced the therapist for utterly failing to empathize with her state or to understand what *her* priorities were and what mattered to *her*. How dare the therapist interpose *his* issue of her anger? *She* was not here to look after him! She had urgently needed to move on to her next concern and the therapist had over-ridden her. Frances felt utterly let down, dropped. She would come back for one more session and only one. That would be the end. Which it was.

Instead of these comments that probed their feelings, for both Beth and Frances "analytic understanding" needed rather to become the medium that they could inhabit. Then the therapist discerns how he is being used, and what he is *for,* but refrains from interpreting all this aloud. Becoming then more invisible, the therapist is able to receive, absorb—to mirror—the patient, to allow air to circulate, to help her breathe more easily.

This necessary cloaking of "analytic understanding", especially at points of extreme indignation, as with Beth and Frances, confirms Winnicott's belief that it is better to wait until the phase is over, and then discuss with the patient what has been happening. Applying also his comment that the analyst's insistence on cleverly discovering a coherent theme may be failing the patient's primary need to be free to communicate nonsense (Winnicott, 1971, p. 56) could prevent such exchanges from turning into a battleground over who has control of the subject matter.

Such a freeing of expression resonates both with Lacan's: "the less you understand, the better you listen" (Lacan, 1960, p. 229). and with the post-structuralist Roland Barthes's comment on the act of reading texts. Barthes argues that we should not try to get "behind" the work—"there is nothing there" (Belsey, pp. 18–20). Instead—and, in the context of Beth's complaint at her therapist's alleged "text book interpretations", as well as the assumption by Frances that the therapist was putting his own issues before hers—the therapist might have applied to the therapy Barthes's advice on the reading of texts: "the space of writing is to be *ranged* over and not *pierced*" (*ibid.*).

In this more freely associative mode together, patient and therapist range over the infinite space of the finite session, where the unfolding process itself constitutes interpretation. Further, as outlined in Chapter One, silent meaning-making and interpretation, as well as speaking aloud, is as busy for the patient as for the therapist. Whenever a slippery feeling gets defined by a word in the person's mind, even at the level of silent but verbal thoughts, the unconscious has already spoken. The act of speaking aloud is then itself already an interpretation. To "range over and not pierce" the space of speaking may indeed suffice.

Perhaps, then, the therapist's pointing out fresh perspectives, links, patterns in the form of "further" or "deeper" meanings "behind" or "beneath" the patient's words and behaviour is not necessarily the main quarry. That kind of meaning-making presupposes a hierarchy of surface and depth that can obscure the fact that "deeper" or "further", "surface" and "depth" are, after all, themselves metaphors, no matter how illuminating. They cannot serve as a literal description of the mind's hidden functioning.

The process of free association need not necessarily involve hunting for the unconscious behind or beneath the words and images. The unconscious is more revealed than concealed in the words that get spoken. In the terminology of Lacan, meanings are multiple, gliding along the surface, in the endless slipping of signifieds beneath the signifier, unable to be tied down to single underlying definitions. His declaration: "the unconscious is structured like a language" (Evans, 1996, p. 218) is reversible—"language is structured like the unconscious". The whole range of literary rhetorical devices and tropes therefore join Freud's list of how the unconscious reveals itself. And this is a formidable list, including not only "dreams, forgettings, misrememberings, jokes, symptoms, verbal and physical mannerisms, parapraxes, but equally metaphor, metonymy, questions, exclamations, demands, 'Freudian slips'" (Bowie, 1982, p. 118). All these are small slits in the unconscious.

For Lacan, there is a kind of inversion of conscious and unconscious, which is reflected further in his conversion of Freud's "where id was, there shall ego be" into "where ego was, there shall id be". Lacan's further gloss on this is "Here, in the field of the dream, you are at home" (Lacan, 1982, p .140).

The manifest material of a session thus appears on a par with the material of asleep dreams: in both sessions and dreams, the misguided efforts of the officious ego are relegated. Like dreams while asleep, therapy sessions become dwelling places as much as sites for deconstruction—an emphasis echoed in one post-Jungian view that the entire therapeutic event should be treated as a dream: "The dream is not in the patient and something he or she does or makes; the patient is in the dream and is doing or being made by its fiction . . ." (Hillman, 1983, p. 45).

This view links meaning-making with playing and free association, in possible contrast with games, where both therapist and patient have their own agenda, heading towards closure. What this playing crucially implies is the conceptualization of, and the therapist's acceptance of, "formlessness"

For the fostering of this non-purposive being, the patient must be allowed to communicate a succession of ideas, impulses and sensations not necessarily linked ... There is room for the idea of unrelated thought sequences, which the analyst will do well to accept as such, not assuming the existence of a significant thread. [Winnicott, 1971, p. 55]

The idea of such fluidity on the borders of consciousness, where the keynote is "being:" rather than "doing", suggests, perhaps unwittingly, the kind of "stream-of-consciousness" that even James Joyce and Virginia Woolf might have died for. I think that the process of free association, of "non-purposive being", actually seems closest to the stream-of-*consciousness* striven for in modernist experimental writing. As claimed by the philosopher Galen Strawson, Joyce made

his mindstreams too consequential: every one of his characters' thought-contents can be made sense of in the light of what has gone before or the external surroundings. One thing leads too much to another, however oddly. Joyce's rendering of consciousness is just not messy enough. [Strawson, 2002]

Strawson, however, describes a model of Free Association that defies such structure and order:

For most people, inner thought is broken and hiccupy. There are gaps and fadings and fugues. It seizes up, it flies off, it suddenly flashes with extraneous matter. It fits Dan Dennett's "Pandemonium" model of the mind-brain, which depicts not-yet-conscious words, ideas, mood-tones, thoughts, impulses of all sorts jostling competitively for emergence into consciousness. [Strawson, 2002]

The branching pattern in the following illustration, the movement of free association between participants in psychotherapy appears more anarchic, less seamless than is sometimes implied in fictional "stream-of-consciousess" material.

Max—demons or daemons?

A patient, struggling to convey to the therapist the nature of his inner "dementor"—a figure from the Harry Potter books—was rejecting the therapist's analogy with a squalling, unappeasable infant. Max insisted that this alien tenant was no way like a baby; "It's a *demon*", he suddenly shuddered.

The therapist voiced the association that immediately came to her consciousness: that of Philip Pullman's trilogy *His Dark Materials*: 'Rather than your *demon*, I would like to be able to give you your *daemon*, which you do also have. But I think you feel severed from this daemon."

In the mythology of Philip Pullman, the daemon is a kind of live transitional object, an extension of the self in the form of an initially shape-shifting creature, which settles into its appropriate final form when its human counterpart grows up. These daemons are the externalized part of each individual self, with whom there is perpetual communion. So compelling is the vision of this idyllic relationship with one's daemon that the reader is no less appalled than the child heroine, Lyra, on discovering the sacrilege of sinister scientific experiments to *sever* children from their daemons.

The patient, Max, steeped in this mythology, seized on his therapist's reference to "severed". "*That* is the word! When that dementor's around, I am severed from myself." This sequence points to the independent path of free association: the fortuitous concept of "severed" captured and defined precisely the dire feeling of Max's relationship to his "dementor". The utterance of the word "severed" is what afforded more immediate relief and clarification than the potentially fruitful visualization of the life-giving *daemon*. But beyond this, without overtly responding to the therapist's "offer" of the *daemon*, there were new possibilities. At a less conscious level, a potential space was hollowed out for the more benign presence of the *daemon* in the patient's psyche and a prospective weakening of the dementor's grip.

In a more seamless sequence, the patient might have picked up directly on the consoling alternative of *daemon* to demon and elaborated on its value for him. Instead, what grabbed him was the word "severed", which came to the therapist through her association with the horrifying surgical severing of the daemon from its human counterpart. In such transitional moments, playing as freedom of association thus involves being both together and separate within the appointed space–time, where what occurs evolves organically in a network of spoken and unspoken communication.

This playing approach to listening and interpreting lowers the therapist from his or her pedestal. Meaning-making becomes a shared activity, with overt interpretation lying as much with the patient as with the analyst, within the shared or overlapping space for playing. It is a network of spoken and unspoken communication, shared and separate, by both patient and therapist. Within the set-apart space and time, the patient and therapist are in some measure creations of each other, not separate entities, and without wholly autonomous "inner realities" that can be *objectively* observed by either party. In the same way that "there is no such thing as an infant" (Winnicott, 1965, p. 39), there is no such thing as a patient or an analyst.

CHAPTER SEVEN

No-space: psychotic meaning-making and regression

E motional and psychological disturbance brings a narrowing of the space between symbol and symbolized, which is reflected in a narrowing of the space between patient and therapist. Symbol and symbolized can become fused together in a reversion to the more magical thinking of symbolic equation (cf. Chapter One). Here, both difference and similarity get swallowed up in sameness. Symbolic equation entails the loss—however briefly—of the "as if", metaphorical element, both in words and situations.

This is famously illustrated by the example of Hannah Segal's two disturbed musicians. (Segal, 1983, p. 265). The first, a concert violinist, was conscious of his instrument's sexual symbolism and of masturbatory fantasies, but his playing was unaffected by it. But the second musician, a schizophrenic, refused to play his violin because he insisted that he could not "masturbate in public". The action of playing "equalled" masturbation. The violin *was* the penis. Segal comments:

> That kind of mature symbolisation of the first violinist is like a process of the completion of mourning; the object is given up and

symbolised in other ways. But my schizophrenic never gave up certain things and concretely wanted to find the penis in the violin.

This mode of thought may arise during phases of high dependence or regression in therapy. As the space between patient and therapist narrows, so thinking becomes more primitive. Indeed, Winnicott, writing extensively on these states, refers to them as "psychotic". Applying his concept of a transitional space between mother and baby to the therapeutic relationship, the patient moves in and out of tentative separateness to states of merging with the analyst—like "now you see a space, now you don't". Winnicott refers to meeting such regressive patterns by unconditionally playing the part demanded by the patient:

> The couch and the pillows are there for the patient's use. They will appear in ideas and dreams and then will stand for the analyst's body, breast, arms, hands etc., in an infinite variety of ways. In so far as the patient is regressed [for a moment or for an hour or over a long period of time] the couch is the analyst, the pillows are breasts, the analyst is the mother at a certain past era. In the extreme it is no longer true to say of the couch that the couch *represents* the analyst; the couch *is* the analyst. [Winnicott, 1954, p. 288, italics added]

So here, for Winnicott is no question of *interpreting* to the patient his/her demand. Rather, by unconditionally fulfilling the role laid upon him, he accepts a suspension of their negotiated distance. Entering into the spirit of the patient's need, he turns symbolic equation into a therapeutic tool, hopefully containing the regression within the analytic hour:

> Acting out has to be tolerated in this sort of work, and with the acting out in the analytic hour the analyst will find it necessary to play a part, although usually in token form. [*ibid.*, p. 289]

But in contrast to this evocation of an ideal attunement between patient and therapist, if a patient feels unheard or misunderstood, this shifting space between patient and therapist becomes a gulf. In any such deterioration of trusting feelings towards the therapist, the patient clings more tightly to the life-raft of the therapist's words, past and present. Words and sayings are plucked from their original context, quoted back at the therapist as a sacred, once and for all oracle. Or the therapist's words have given such offence that they are irredeemable and no reconciliation is possible.

This brings a flavour of symbolic equation where the words of the therapist are isolated from both their original context and their original emotional tenor and turned into absolutes, welded to a single, immovable meaning.

Dominic—kicking the cat

The following case report illustrates the apparently immutable meaning of words, focusing in this case on the word "relationship".

Dominic, a fierce young poet, new to psychotherapy, informed his therapist that he had now told her everything about himself. What was supposed to happen next? The therapist replied, "All we have, then, is our relationship". For the young man, this was revelatory and highly exciting. His latent transference feelings for the therapist became passionate and when she introduced a cautionary note, commenting, "For you, this is like being in love", this symbolic "like"—"as if"— dimension was lost on Dominic. For him, this was *the same* as being in love.

Although in practice observing the negotiated space between them, it was a sore trial to him. After long focus on the transference relationship, the therapist tried to steer the therapy elsewhere, asking the patient what more he might want from his therapy. She was strangely unprepared for Dominic's immediate reply, "Some form of physical contact", and not sufficiently experienced to convert the sexual demand into the regressive need, as described above, by Winnicott.

When the patient expressed dissatisfaction with the therapist's behaviour, mentioning her original reference to their "relationship" he was appalled at her dismissive reply. She seemed to be speaking about quite other people, as if in quotation marks: "Well . . . 'relationship' or 'treatment' or 'work' . . . whatever . . .'

This apparent *volte face* pulled the rug from under Dominic's feet. The gulf between the patient and therapist was potentially unbridgeable in terms of the fixity and absoluteness of an utterance for one, regardless of context, and for the other the apparent fluidity of a contract, which had a largely symbolic basis. All that took place was to be seen as relative and provisional—as shown by her plainly defensive reaction. In the trajectory of that single word "relationship" can be traced the decline of this therapy.

Dominic's fierce attachment to that concept "relationship", as bred in the therapy, was followed by an even stronger rejection of newly unacceptable words from the therapist. On one occasion, arriving with a pleasant greeting, Dominic announced to the therapist, with some gusto, that, driving off in his car after the previous session, he had suddenly realized that she had ended ten minutes early. But at once he had understood that this was because she had failed to remember the newly arranged timing of their sessions. He assured the therapist that he hadn't at all minded this mistake. In fact, knowing the reason, he had felt amused, continuing, "What I want to talk about now is my angry feelings towards my cat, Amogga. I feel such a fury with her when she hisses in fear of me." To the therapist's question as to whether the cat had any reason to be afraid, Dominic replied that he "kicked her around", and that his father had once ill-treated another family cat.

He then reported how, again after the previous foreshortened session, he had a violent dream of rage with his father. In the dream, Dominic, perched on the car bonnet, had smashed his way into the car and killed his father, ripping out his organs and flinging them into the road. He asserted, 'Although not my actual father, I knew the figure in the dream stood for him, just as in an earlier dream, the man represented *you*."

The therapist suggested, "Perhaps he also stood for me again in this dream." Dominic hotly denied this. But instead of dropping it, the therapist chose to retrace the drift of Dominic's remarks so far: from the truncated last session to anger towards the cat, to the dream of murdering his father; and even to his reference to the therapist from an earlier dream. Perhaps he had, after all, at some level, been angry about the missing ten minutes from last time and hence the violent dream that night?

Dominic now became enraged, and no matter how willing the therapist was to withdraw her rejected observation, Dominic could not forgive her claim to have seen those links in his material. Her offence acquired a granite absoluteness and immutability. Despite repeated glimpses of a rapprochement, the incident would suddenly loom up and glower in intractable solidity, leading to further sterile inquests.

The whole tone of this encounter suggests that the patient was experiencing too great a gulf between himself and the therapist.

Her offending interpretation, instead of giving illumination humil-
iated him, because she claimed—wrongly in his eyes—to have seen
what he had not seen. With his seething anger and aggression, he
engineered a compensating clash futilely designed to close the
widening gulf between them.

Possibly if the therapist had instead picked up on the transference–countertransference hints in the terrified female cat, Amogga,
the patient would have felt more contained ... He needed to see
that the mother/therapist was fearless and well able to hold him.
For perhaps all this upheaval signalled the need for "the analyst to
be the mother at a certain past era", which, in contrast to the
Winnicott evocation above (Winnicott, 1954, p. 288), she signally
failed to be.

On the one hand, then, when there is a reversion towards
symbolic equation, towards more juvenile, concrete, ways of meaning-making, as outlined in Chapter One—cow is called "cow"
because it has horns—the patient loses a sense of the contextuality
and provisionality of any exchange. Any insight into the ephemeral
nature of words has vanished in the *binding to himself a joy* rather
than *kissing the joy as it flies*

> He who binds to himself a joy
> does the winging life destroy.
> He who kisses the joy on its flight
> Lives in eternity's sunlight.
>
> [William Blake]

On the other hand, given the patient's sense of vulnerability, the
therapist needs to watch his/her words and guard against careless
inconsistency. For it is not least the illusion of stable, fixed meanings, deriving from the "cow=horn" era of development that has
been sustaining the patient. And now, in the gulf between the
couple, those meanings seem invalidated—the therapist's words
prove to be dud food.

Jeremiah Solomon

The following material demonstrates a more psychotic relationship
to meanings, where the person's thought linkages correspond to

full blown symbolic equation. In the inappropriate meanings and false links forged, there occurs a total abolition of space between symbol and symbolized. Particularly striking in the sequence presented is the unmistakable origin of the thought disorder in an emotional deficit, which renders Jeremiah's sense of self wholly insecure and dependent on the affirmation of others.

Like Hannah Segal's duo, Jeremiah Solomon was another gifted musician, but in certain moods his violin became equated with a malevolent and threatening rival. After a concert performance he would feel depleted, envious, abandoned, because all the applause had been for the violin. He was merely the compliant instrument, the "vessel through which the music pours", as Stravinsky described it. On two occasions he smashed his instrument on the pavement.

> In Jeremiah's first therapy session at a psychotherapy unit, the disturbance in his thought patterns emerged in an overriding concern with names. He expressed immediate relief that the doctor–therapist addressed him as "Jeremiah", rather than "Jerry" and that she had "used the right tone of voice" [unlike his mother and the psychiatrist.]. "My relationship with people depends entirely on how they say my name and on their tone of voice. From how they say my name I can tell everything they think. And only if my name is pronounced in a certain way do I feel sufficiently approved of to relate to a person. I get furious with my sister and mother for saying 'Jerry'. And although you said your name was X, only if I address you with your full title, Dr X Y, can I give you your proper reverence."

> Jeremiah was thus wholly identified with, and not merely represented by, his full name, as was the doctor by hers. On one occasion, when Jeremiah was late for his session, and the doctor was waiting in the office, she saw Jeremiah come in to the building and said to the receptionist, "Oh, here he is!" Jeremiah heard this and, once in the consulting room, grew incandescent with rage that Dr X should have degraded him in this manner—i.e. by failing to say to the receptionist, "Here is Mr Jeremiah Solomon."

> By a system of metonymic substitution, bare names bore all the imagined qualities of their subjects in an abolition of any intermediate spaces. Contact with the therapist, with any other person, as "another" was too dangerous, too intrusive. All encounters therefore had to occur through osmosis and absorption, achieved by a private system of "logic", which ensured a simultaneous necessary distance.

So Jeremiah detoxified individuals by computerization, by classifying them almost solely in terms of race, geographical origin, and gender. Whether they came from Barnet or Kent, Brisbane or Kenya, determined their character, as did length of residence in a place. "You can't expect so much of a family who've only been here forty years. They're not indigenous." With the abolition in Jeremiah's mind of any distinction between the generic and the particular, having once disliked one individual from Kent, he denounced anyone else from there as bound to possess the same faults.

The mode of meaning-making displayed by Jeremiah Solomon moves closer to the "inflationary increases of significances", applied by Thomas Sass to schizoid and schizophrenic states (Sass, 1996). In the symbolic edifice on which Jeremiah leaned, there appear to be tinges both of more extreme schizophrenic conditions and of autistic thinking. Indeed, Jeremiah enjoyed the distinction of defying all psychiatric attempts to agree on a diagnosis of his condition.

Jeremiah's material confirms the view of most contemporary psychoanalysis and of neuro-scientific research, that disturbed reasoning is inextricably intertwined with disorders of feeling, interfering with the capacity for relating to others. This recognition is a spur to both psychotherapy and psychiatry to the decisive relocation of the patient from a position of *object*, observed for his/her bizarre reasoning, to a position of *subject*, whose feelings in the analytic relationship must be engaged with.

In more crippling psychotic illness the dynamic between distance and merging, between the concrete and the symbolic, is even more pronounced. Although the mode of symbolic equation is classified, especially in psychiatry, as "concrete" thinking, it actually entails a parallel corresponding magnification of ideas with complex symbolic systems.

This is indelibly exemplified in Madame Sechehaye's *Symbolic Realisation*, where, for the seriously ill psychotic young woman, Renée, Sechehaye abandoned analytic interpretation in favour of cooperating with Renée's own obsessive symbolic system. Combined with taking Renée into her home to live, and supporting a full regression, the treatment worked so well that the girl recovered sufficiently to publish her own fascinating account, now sadly out of print, of her illness and its treatment.

The context of the following extract is Renée's convalescence on a farm to which Sechehaye had been sending top quality apples from town:

> I was led to modify the psychoanalytic treatment, in order to reach the patient's emotions, and help her out of the walled enclosure of her unreality. The simplest means of contact which I used was *to realise the unconscious desire, according to the symbolism presented by the patient.* I would like to stress already now that the symbols were reality to the patient—in fact, the only reality; they were symbols merely for the analyst.

> Renée runs away [from the farm where she was convalescing] and arrives at my house all alone at night, in terrible agony. I persist in trying to understand the symbolism of the apples. To the remark that I had given her as many [fine] apples as she wanted, Renée cries: "Yes, but those are store apples, apples for big people, but I want apples from Mummy, like that," pointing to my breasts. "Those apples there, Mummy gives them only when one is hungry." I understand at last what must be done! Since the apples represent maternal milk, I must give them to her like a mother feeding her baby: I must give her the symbol myself, directly and without intermediary—and at a fixed hour. To verify my hypothesis I carry it out at once. Taking an apple, and cutting it in two I offer Renée a piece, saying, "It is to drink the milk from Mummy's apples, Mummy is going to give it to you." Renée then leans up against my shoulder, presses the apple on my breast, and very solemnly, with intense happiness, eats it.

> The symbolism of the apples was the revival of all the shocks that Renée had had in infancy in regard to food, which represents maternal love. First of all, the mother had put so much water in the milk that it had hardly had any consistency at all and could not satisfy the child. [Sechehaye, 1951, p. 44]

What is revealed here with such clarity is how "the symbols were reality to the patient—in fact, the only reality". Without this evidence, one might have expected Renée to refer to Mother Sechehaye's apple as the "milk" it actually represented for her. Instead, she insists on " '*apples* from Mummy, like that', pointing to my breasts. 'Those apples there, Mummy gives them only when one is hungry'."

Thus, investment has been wholly transferred from the object—milk—to its representation: *apple*. The apple has become so absolutely equated with the milk in the symbolic system that Renée constructed and inhabits that the reality of milk is displaced. Thus, symbolic breast feeding with a feeding bottle of milk would not have done at all because only the apple is "real" milk. It is this reality of the apple symbol at Sechehaye's breast that is needed. So we are shown a further stage in the process of symbolic equation, where the source of the symbol—mother's milk—is wholly displaced by the symbol itself.

In relation to how language is used in modes of symbolic equation, I refer again to the precedence taken by interpreting the world to oneself over the act of communication with others, as introduced in Chapter One. Both the Jeremiah Solomon and—still more—the Renée material are extreme examples of the inner interpretative activity, conscious and unconscious, for which any outward expression or spoken communication is only the tip of the iceberg. What inner processes must occur to generate these complex symbolic systems prior to their being voiced?

Viewing the descent into symbolic equation in terms of the shifting spaces both between the participants and between word and meaning, in Renée's case we see what might look like an unequalled merging between patient and analyst–mother. Not only is there no-space *between* symbol and symbolized, but the apple-as-milk usurps milk-as-milk, giving a flavour of what it must be like to live in a world where the symbol is the reality. It is also fascinating that, in order to balance her fulfilment of Renée's need for 'the analyst to be the mother at a certain past era' (Winnicott, 1954, p. 288), acting as a *literal* nurturing mother, each morning Madame Sechehaye would also give Renée a set-apart analytic hour, which modelled the gradual restoration of a potential space between the couple.

The annihilation of space manifested in symbolic equation assumes another guise in autistic states. While it is beyond my brief to engage in the vast domain of autism and issues of its aetiology, two particular features of autism offer a further variation on the phenomenon of space and no-space in autistic thought and communication. These features shed further light on the relationship between space and meaning-making.

As already seen, the capacity for healthy symbolization presupposes a gap between word and object, signifier and signified. But many people on the autistic spectrum do not occupy a three-dimensional world of time and space in which the intertwining of thought and feeling can proceed. Instead they may inhabit a flat, two-dimensional world, where sound and *sensation* (Maiello, 1997, p. 1ff) take the place of feeling and thought; where, instead of contact with another, there is only a sticky adhesiveness.

This symptom of sticky adhesiveness, accompanied by frequent dependence on, and addiction to, hard, often small objects, contrasts with the dance of separateness and fusion visualized by Winnicott, Stern, and Trevarthen as the hallmark of transitional space and an emerging symbolic capacity. Thus, instead of fluidity of movement in space–time, a severely autistic person is stuck between a rock and a soft place.

In *Live Company*, Alvarez evokes her own confusion arising from an initial unawareness that there was no-space between her and her patient, Robbie. You could say she was duped by the sense of a great distance between herself and this "attractive child, with an uncoordinated, floppy, boneless look about him. He came into the playroom in a very lost and bewildered state, muttering 'gone' and looking frightened" (Alvarez, 1992a, p. 16). This apparent distance bolstered Anne Alvarez's assumption, based on her theoretical background and personal practice, that Robbie would possess live, active feelings—fears/desires—which he would naturally express, "put into" her. Gradually, she concluded that he wanted nothing, there was scarcely a "he" there to do the wanting—little more than a flaccid passivity. And, as for "projecting into her", there was no-space for "projection"—for throwing across—because Robbie was stuck in a gluey adhesion to his therapist (*ibid.*).

A glimmer of vitality occurred when Robbie "picked up a little arched brick and said 'bridge'"; but this was countered by a more pathological pleasure in getting entangled in a long ball of string, which he called being "stuck". Finally, he handed Alvarez a piece of plasticine asking her to "make it soft". These three elements— hardness of the brick, softness of the plasticine and the stuck entanglement of the string served as reference points in the years of treatment, when for so long the "bridge" was eclipsed by the "stuckness", the sticky adhesiveness, and the pursuit of "softness".

The eventual advent of space between Robbie and Alvarez, when he saw her, seemingly for the first time, as a distinct person, was triggered by an impending lengthy break:

> While I was talking, he had been shaking his hands and dispersing all his distress and anger in the ineffectual and draining way I have described before. Suddenly he stopped, came over and examined my face with great tenderness, then the area of my breast and then said, slowly, "Hello," almost as though he'd just recognised an old friend he hadn't seen for ten years. [Alvarez, 1992a, p. 30]

If meaning-making and projection were originally lacking in this child, terror was not, as an account slowly emerged of his long captivity in a bottomless dark well. Without his entangling adhesive manoeuvres he dreaded being sucked down for ever. This is the relationship to the "black hole", which Frances Tustin defines as a gap or hole in the fabric of one's being. It is this hole that substitutes for the evolving space necessary for symbolic activity. In the valuable collection of tributes to Tustin, as one of the great pioneers of the field, it is suggested that "Tustin's theories speak to the origins of semiotic processes". In these essays it is also claimed that Tustin's patients were mostly "high level" autists who would now be classified as having Asperger's syndrome, (Grotstein, 1997, p. 257f.)

Individuals with Asperger's, unlike Anne Alvarez's Robbie in his early years of treatment, are gripped not only by intense and unmanageable extremes of emotion, but also partake of highly strange symbolic activity. This is fascinatingly illustrated by the case of twelve-year-old Elly, who graduated from the "ordering principles" of reliance on shapes of bodily substances to "numbers", which produced "nice" or "nasty" sensations. Some numbers aroused such

> "rapture" . . . that they were unutterable: Elly could only write them. The moon was number 7 for Elly . . . On the nights following a full moon, it rises outside Elly's window and stays for several hours partly visible behind a large tree . . . she will not say its name but will refer to "something behind the tree" . . . If the moon is obscured, Elly lies in bed and cries her tearless autistic cry. [Tustin, 1986, p. 129]

PART TWO

THE STRUGGLE
BETWEEN MASKS

He and She

As the moon sidles up
Must she sidle up,
As trips the scared moon
Away must she trip:
"His light had struck me blind
Dared I stop."

She sings as the moon sings:
"I am I, am I;
The greater grows my light
The further that I fly."
All creation shivers
With that sweet cry.

W. B. Yeats

CHAPTER EIGHT

The mask of language

For both Lacan and Winnicott, building on Freud's theory of the Oedipus complex, symbolic development is tied to inner upheavals. As considered in Chapters Two and Three, these relate to the potentially painful realization of the m/other's otherness. It is the baby's growing awareness of space–time, of "thirdness"—of "fatherness"—that assists this realisation of "twoness", of difference. Such awareness occurs, I believe, whether there is only one actual "other" in the baby's life or twenty-one others.

As outlined in Chapter One, the advent of a third/father, is linked to the discovery of *difference,* as carved out by language. It is awareness of *He and She,* which is seen by Lacan, in his version of the oedipal drama, as the basis of all other distinctions. From this primary scent of difference between one gender and the other and between one word and another, comes recognition of self and other and of others within the self..

The Oedipus drama—consciousness of difference—hollows out a sense of lack, of something missing in all human beings. Plato's "desire and pursuit of the whole" is one trademark of being alive. How this perceived wound in nature is regarded in psychoanalysis, is clarified by the literary theorist, Terry Eagleton:

For the drama of the Oedipus complex to come about at all, the child must . . . have become dimly aware of sexual difference. It is the entry of the father which signifies this sexual difference . . . It is only when by accepting the necessity of sexual difference, of distinct gender roles, that the child, who has previously been unaware of such problems, can become properly "socialised". Lacan's originality is to rewrite this process, which we have already seen in Freud's account of the Oedipus complex, in terms of language. . . . With the entry of the father, the child . . . now has to grasp Saussure's point that identities come about only as a result of difference—that one term or subject is only what it is by excluding another. Significantly, the child's first discovery of sexual difference occurs at about the same time that it is discovering language itself. [Eagleton, 1985, pp. 165–166]

For Winnicott, as discussed in Chapter Three, the problem of this drama is eased by the infant's relationship to a transitional object. But Lacan's parallel scene is especially stark and severe. As observed in Chapter Two, for the Lacanian infant, according to some versions, it seems that there is never omnipotence, never the assumption of oneness with the m/other. This infant is born already wounded, already separate and lacking, torn from "itself"—from the infant-as-part-of-the-mother within the womb—by the act of birth. Even the breast may therefore not be wholly blissful. At best, perhaps it is only second best. Then the father/phallus comes along to complete a process begun prior to conception, trawling the child into a bounded symbolic order. It means, from infancy onwards, never to be free of pigeon-holing, from categorization, classification, and named roles, as son/daughter, sibling, grandchild, with the piling on of life's successive positions bringing further modifications to the self. Until language itself is finally floored by the impossibility of the statement, "I am dead". Shaped by language, the individual is a subject *divided* from h/erself, with masking the very condition of becoming conscious.

We could almost say that for Lacan birth itself equals the loss of Eden, while for Winnicott it is language, treated as a later arrival on the scene, that signals Eden's end, the loss of direct, pure communication between mother and baby. This communication is replaced by "various techniques for indirect communication, the most obvious of which is the use of language". (Winnicott, 1963, p. 188). With the cessation of that original direct, pure communication, the spontaneous self-expression of the screaming or smiling baby is modified. The self becomes filtered, increasingly *represented* to others through words, through the medium and mask of language.

In the following poem, Yeats's "The Mask", the mask is celebrated as *itself* the vibrant source of freedom, power, and spoken communication. As a metaphor for how language functions as the self's mediator, here, the speaker's mask acts to show and to hide, to attack and defend:

THE MASK

Put off that mask of burning gold
With emerald eyes.'
"Oh no, my dear, you make so bold
To find if hearts be wild and wise
And yet not cold."

"I would but find what's there to find,
Love or deceit."
"It was the mask engaged your mind
And after set your heart to beat.
Not what's behind."

"But lest you are my enemy
I must enquire."
"Oh no, my dear, let all that be.
What matter, so there is but fire
In you, in me?"

[Jeffares, 1976]

In this dialogue, the first speaker, "she", pleads with the other, "he", to remove his mask, so that she may discover the "real" truth about him: *"I would but find what's there to find, / Love or deceit."* But the other insists that to remove his mask would be to strip away not disguise, but the mainspring, the source of their mutual attraction: *"It was the* mask *engaged your mind / And after set your heart to beat / Not what's behind.'*

The speaker, it seems, is claiming that the mask, the outer representation, is an integral part of himself and the vital means of connection between himself and the other, while the actual patterning of the verse ironically heightens the complexity and ambivalence behind this assertion. For in responding to the other's desire to establish whether this figure is friend or foe: "lest you are my enemy I must enquire", the man's final words of supposed reassurance, "*What matter, so there is but fire/ In you, in me?*" refuses any clear distinction between "mask" and "self".

Thus the mask appears both to liberate and protect the individual, cushioning the perception that any assured sense of identity is constantly undermined and misshapen by the impact of others, of the world, of inner disturbance. In his major poems, plays, and prose works, Yeats assigned to the Mask a still more central place in the patterning both of larger reality and of the individual. He saw the mask as representing all the hidden and opposite facets of the manifest personality, with the self defined as the "struggle between masks" (Unterecker, 1973, p 16).

For Yeats, within every individual, nation and age is hidden all that is opposite to the external appearance. This hidden part must be pursued and nurtured. For in its interaction with the outer part, immense achievement and great strength would result. Here, Yeats closely accords with Jung's view of "psychic wholeness" as . . . "living in a structure within which opposites are at play" (Umbert, 1988, p. 117). Masks, above all the mask of language, thus reveal by concealing, spanning both manifest and hidden, conscious and unconscious levels of experience.

True versus false

Winnicott's potent myth of the development of the False Self bears little resemblance to popular folk-lore that encourages searches for "my true self". For Winnicott, a pathological split of the original self into True and False Self appears to derive from deficient or harmful early nurturing. As depicted in *The Mirror Role of Mother and Family*, poor holding and mirroring drives the deprived baby prematurely back on to its own resources. It then becomes its own mirror, its own nurse, the watcher and predictor of its mother's moods:

> [in] the case of the baby whose mother reflects her own mood or, worse still, the rigidity of her own defences . . . what does the baby

see? . . . many babies . . . do have to have a long experience of not
getting back what they are giving. [Winnicott, 1971, p. 112]

It is this lack of that steady affirmation depicted in Chapter Two,
that for Winnicott, leads to an early splitting of the self into True and
False, where the False Self, with its hallmark, compliance, acts as
caretaker for the True Self. His extended application of the concept,
True and False Self, covers a range of psychic states. These feature at
one extreme the severely schizoid or split predicament of feeling
unreal, un-alive, not knowing how to be. "Falseness" here implies
that the individual is cut off from the vital mainspring of his/her
being. At the other extreme, "false" becomes a contradictory reference by Winnicott to more "healthy" forms of splitting as in the
"Falseness—self-representation—of necessary social functioning:

> In health: the False Self is represented by the whole organisation of
> the polite and mannered social attitude, a "not wearing the heart on
> the sleeve", as might be said. Much has gone to the individual's
> ability to forego omnipotence and the primary process in general,
> the gain being the place in society which can never be attained or
> maintained by the True Self alone. [Winnicott, 1965, p. 143]

Thus, the original involuntary, forced, defensive position shades
here into something almost free and almost chosen. Something,
indeed, akin to the Jungian concept of "persona" or social mask,
which bears far fewer negative connotations than the term "false
self". It is this overloading of the false self metaphor that leads me
to introduce the conceit of Free Masks and Forced Masks. For this
necessary "falseness" in health, I believe that this plural metaphor
of "forced masks versus free masks" is more useful than that of an
implied single "split" into True and False. Furthermore, beyond
their making sense of the individual as victim of early damage, the
notion of forced masks sheds light on later disturbance arising
despite good-enough early experience.

In that original faulty maternal mirroring, it is as if the child's
face is stuck with the mother's face like a forced mask. Here, when
the person's early mirroring is too misty for the self to be reflected
back; or where there is some basic defect in the personality; or,
indeed, where there have been severe later traumas: all these are
possible sources of forced masks, or an *array* of forced masks.

The conceit of forced masks and free masks accommodates the need that persists throughout life for positive mirroring. For despite sound early mirroring and the increasing repertoire of masks arising freely from within, there is no guarantee against the later cracking of an original affirming reflection. Further, it becomes increasingly the mirroring of *others,* apart from the m/other and other main carers, that contributes to the psychic health of the individual. As the child grows older, like the patient in therapy, mirroring will not imply a ceaselessly uncritical, approving reflecting back. For both the developing child and the therapy patient, the presence of free masks depends on exposure not only to the affirmation of others, but also to a measure of *critical* mirroring. The idea of a *range* of masks elicited by one's own shifting moods and by the kaleidoscopic interplay of oneself and the world suggests the individual's fluidity and plurality—if not simply the fashionably named "bundle of impressions" of popular science.

A suggestion of "forced masks" as endemic to the human condition appears also in Lacan's myth of the Mirror stage. The child's joyous first recognition of itself in the mirror as a whole, coordinated being, is seen as a trap and a trick. In its very act of freely, but mistakenly, identifying itself with its seemingly ideal reflection, a mask is clamped upon the child, which will thereafter mislead him/her into lifelong false identifications.

Evolving, therefore, both from the Lacanian infant's misrecognition of itself in the mirror and the Winnicottian infant's seminal experience of maternal mirroring towards awareness of difference, language can be seen as a basic mask of the personality. To be born an heir to language is a mighty inheritance. It is also to be an heir to masks, both forced and free.

CHAPTER NINE

Forced masks and free masks

"A work of art also masks its desires through the 'disguise' by which many elements of aesthetic form distract the audience"

(Freud, 1908e, pp. 141–153)

P sychoanalysis and theatre are united in the belief that desire is the basic force behind both activities. For Stanislavsky, a complete drama comprised successive, linked units each informed by an "underlying objective" of the characters, which actors must formulate in terms of "*I want to . . .*". Thus the actor's own desire to fulfil his/her role fuels the desire generated in his/her "character". This interplay produces the fictionalization of desire, as implied by Freud's point above that "a work of art also masks its desires through the 'disguise' by which many elements of aesthetic form distract the audience". Freud is suggesting that desire is not only a driving force, but is also distanced as an *object* held up for observation when it aspires to the condition of art. This aesthetic objectifying of desire opposes any threat of its engulfing the participants. Paradoxically, then, the "disguise" of desire contributes to that necessary space between actor and audience, therapist and patient, serving as a primary protective and liberating mask.

Theatrical masks

The action of theatrical masks, both metaphorical and literal, further highlights the extraordinarily complex relationship between forced masks and free masks in the meaning-making process.

In a Radio Three series on role play, the actor Eileen Atkins recalls the epilogue of Shaw's *St Joan*, when the resurrected Joan returns to visit the Dauphin, and all those who betrayed Joan to the flames return, one by one, expressing remorse at her death by burning.

During one performance a young man from the audience, unkempt, in ragged jeans and yellow tee shirt, leapt up on the stage and joined the costumed actors around Joan. As, one by one, each character in the play once more rejected the saint and sadly withdrew, the demented-looking youth knelt down in front of Atkins, vowing, "*I'll* never leave you, Joan." At first, Atkins the actor felt completely disorientated by this *deus ex machina*. But then she found herself laying her hand on the youth's head, and together they rose, holding hands, to face the audience. As Atkins saw the youth's face, she realized she recognized him as a once promising young actor who had lost his way. The audience and critics were in raptures at this supposedly planned, inspired, and moving "updating" of the original play.

The case of the confused youth leaping on to the stage and vowing allegiance to the actor in her role as Joan is a graphic example of the simultaneous presence of both *forced* masks and free masks, of competing or co-existent truths. His psychosis and misidentification suggest the domain of forced masks associated with scars in the personality. But, like the reified figure in Beckett's *Catastrophe,* who performed an autonomous act by disobediently raising his head at the end of the play (cf. Chapter Four), the complex tangle of '"forced" and "free" appears in the youth's freely mounting the stage and freely speaking his wholly appropriate line, "I'll never leave you, Joan." Which mask(s) was he wearing at that moment? Had he, once more, become the original professional actor playing his part? Or was his Joan a "real" miraculous saint, capable of restoring his disturbed self to mental health? Was the whole act a stunt to regain theatrical recognition? And what further masks might have been in play in an incident where different masks, different forms of truth collide and intertwine? So perhaps the model of forced masks and free masks that does most justice to such complexity is a plurality, maybe a continuum of masks, a jumble of forced masks and free masks.

How free, then are the masks voluntarily embraced by the actor? Demands made on actors by the Stanislavsky approach to their roles and their relationship to the other characters (followed also in American Method Acting and in the work of Mike Leigh) involve the assumption of a mask, which wholly "covers" their face, a total dedication to embracing the "truth" of their role and becoming possessed by it. Stanislavsky expressively conveys the nature and paradox of this kind of mask in his account of Kostya, a drama student, who has been told to put on character make-up, but nothing satisfies him. He creams his face to remove the greasepaint and then, unexpectedly

> All the colours blurred . . . It was difficult to distinguish where my nose was, or my eyes or my lips. I smeared some of the same cream on my beard and moustache and then finally all over my wig. Some of the hair clotted into lumps . . . and then, almost as if I were in a delirium, I trembled, my heart pounded, I did away with my eyebrows, powdered myself at random, smeared the back of my hands with a greenish colour and the palms with a light pink. I did all this with a quick, sure touch, for this time I knew who I was representing, and what kind of fellow he was!

> [He then paced the room feeling] how all the parts of my body, features, facial lines, fell into their proper places, and established themselves . . . I glanced in the mirror and did not recognise myself. Since I had looked into it the last time a fresh transformation had taken place in me. "It is he, it is he", I exclaimed . . .

> He presents himself to the director (Tortsov), introducing himself as "the critic". He's surprised to find his body doing things by itself, things he hadn't intended. "Quite unexpectedly my twisted leg came out in advance, I raised my top hat with careful exaggeration and executed a polite bow. [Stanislavsky, 1979, p. 16]

Stanislavsky concludes, "A characterisation is the mask which hides the actor individual. Protected by it, he can lay bare his soul to the last intimate detail" (Stanislavsky, 1979, p. 30).

According to this conceit, only by means of the mask "covering" the face can the actor's soul utterly serve the character s/he is playing. The mask's full reality, born of illusion, bears a trueness, that, while mediated by the "soul" of the actor, is nevertheless not identical with it. (Although "soul" is unfashionable and is usually distinguished from the "self", with connotations of immortality, in Stanislavsky's usage "soul" appears synonymous with the idea of one's whole being informing an activity. "Personality" is perhaps the closest contemporary word. But after all, "soul" is the direct translation of "psyche", so "soul" is more central than "self" in analytic work, as depicted in Bettelheim's *Freud and Man's Soul*.) The value of the Stanislavsky mask of the actor's role thus lies in its rendering of truth through disguise and revelation through concealment, with no implication of falseness.

George Devine, the former director of the Royal Court Theatre, in his extraordinary work with actors and literal masks, required the actor to *become* his/her designated Mask. It was quite common for the wearer then to be terrified at the sight of the Mask's reflection in the mirror. The actor's entire personality was subdued to the character of this Mask—the initial is capitalized because Devine would address not the actor but only the Mask, as the "real" person present. The actors were sometimes unable to shed their Mask character at the end of an improvisation session and felt traumatized.

So, for the actor, protected by the mask of his/her character, the goal of "laying bare his soul to the last intimate detail" exacts a price, particularly when free masks become "forced", when full inner possession by their role can leave the actor scarred and marked by its personality and pathology. The distinction between the "innermost" self and its masks is then lost. For example, an actor playing the evil old man in Strindberg's *Ghost Sonata* would "leave the theatre every night with my knees knocking in terror" (Swerling, 1971, p. 23). It is also well known that several years ago Sean Day Lewis, playing Hamlet, fled from the National Theatre stage convinced that Hamlet's father's ghost was an apparition of his own father, C. Day Lewis. In both of these cases, it seemed as if initially free masks turned into forced masks.

How far metaphorical masks also may, in fact, be forced or free and the risks inherent in performance was simulated by the mime, Marcel Marceau. Delighted at first with the imaginary grinning mask he had evoked and pretended to press on to his face, his entire body became increasingly agonized and contorted as he strove in vain to peel off the fixed grinning mask. A mask that Marceau's character began by assuming freely had turned into a forced mask.

The mask(s) of the therapist—"a living double of you" (Pessoa, 1935)

In making a comparison between the masks of the actor and the masks of the therapist, I am not ignoring the essential contrast: the actor usually plays a character other than him or herself, whereas the analyst is (apparently), *playing* no-one. But if the writer–actor Harold Pinter were to play *himself* in a staging of his life as a drama, it would be significant that here was Pinter not just *being* himself, but also *representing* himself. The nature of the event means that Pinter is wearing a mask of Pinter. And however faithful a rendering of Pinter's personality is staged, it has been transformed into a partial fiction, to be experienced simultaneously as story and as fact, as illusion and as reality. It would be not simply a question of whether Pinter was being his natural, "true" self, but whether he achieved an effective *rendering* of that self. The theatre accentuates the point that *representation* of oneself is the issue on the theatrical stage—as, less visibly, on the stage of the world.

Yet here there is no question of "falseness": a paradox which, I think, sheds further light on the function and effect of the therapist. For the therapist's primary protective mask is furnished by those identical conditions that would allow Pinter to perform Pinter. The therapist need do nothing at all for manifold masks to materialize from the specific conditions of the meeting, and from those masks foisted upon her by the patient in the transference. Remaining (in theory) entirely him or herself, the analyst is made available for the multiple roles foisted upon him or her in the transference and for the patient's heightened meaning-making.

For therapeutic approaches that rely on the therapist's personality and intuition as his/her main tool, Stanislavsky's paradoxical

prescription, already quoted, is relevant: "a mask which hides the
. . . individual. Protected by it, he can lay bare his soul to the last
intimate detail." Revelation of the therapist's soul—personality—is
filtered through the mask of his/her role. The elements of the therapeutic frame, especially the impact of the times, the spaces and the
relative positions of patient and therapist ensure his/her simultaneous concealment. S/he is freed by this mask to be spontaneous
with his/her patient. It is therefore strange that soul-searching by
therapists concerning the legitimacy of self-disclosure always seem
to revolve around the question of telling *facts* about the therapist's
life, as if the imparting of "facts" could ever be as potentially risky
as the ceaseless and inescapable self-revelation to the patient of
how s/he operates, how his/her mind works, what s/he *is*. It is the
mask of the set-up that makes him/her relatively safe.

As for approaches where the therapist relies less on his/her soul
and more on theoretically based interventions, there is also an anal-
ogous theatrical mask. While the "Stanislavsky" therapist wears
his/her mask *over* her face to enable communion and shared free
association, the second kind of therapist holds his/her mask *beside*
her face, like Brecht's actors who are required to remain detached
from their roles (Cousins, 1983). Yet Brechtian performances are no
less powerful than those in the style of Stanislavsky, since actors
may be just as effective and compelling without intense inner
involvement, as in the case of Helene Wiegel, the wife of Brecht,
overwhelming the audience by a prolonged grimace of agony in her
performance of Mother Courage.

In practice, we can assume in the therapist an interplay between
the Stanislavsky and the Brechtian kind of masks as elicited by the
patient—not forgetting all those further masks that the patient
needs to fit on to the therapist in order to find in him or her whatever s/he is seeking.

This was brought home to a therapist who saw the need to curb
the associations, links, and interpretations that kept on flowing from
him. In order to give his patient more space, he resolved one day to
adopt a more "detached" and "formal" (Brechtian) stance than his
usual engaged manner. He was struck by the impact on both the
patient and himself. The patient immediately noticed the therapist's
new demeanour and this had a powerful effect on her, eliciting
darker and disturbing material. The therapist felt increasingly

uneasy, partly because there was a sense that this adopted pose was taking him over and partly because of a feeling that he was somehow exploiting, or even abusing, the patient. A freely chosen mask had turned into a forced mask. There is a danger in making prior decisions to behave in a certain way in an activity that needs to proceed in an organic, unfolding fashion.

At times, also, the situation is strained by a patient's extreme expectations of constancy in the therapist. His/her demands on the therapist to be a fixed, unchanging "still point of the turning world", to be singular rather than dual or manifold, cramp the rich variety of the therapist's personality. This could be seen as the plea for a single, immutable mask to spare the patient from experiencing this person as a weather vane. So dependent may s/he be on the therapist's unchanging, consistent behaviour that it is beyond him/her to conceive that today's apparent cool or distant figure is the same person as the warm, accessible figure of yesterday. The impression of inconsistency and contradictory behaviour can be so powerful that the patient magnifies shifts in the therapist's behaviour, even developing horror-film fantasies of twin or triplet rotating therapist characters—a symptom of near psychotic regression to that original paranoid–schizoid stage of splitting the m/other into good and bad objects. Or is the therapist driving the patient crazy? For it may be beyond the patient's immediate capacity to perceive how s/he him/herself might be contributing to any prevailing bad atmosphere . . .

CHAPTER TEN

Child's play: show and hide

I n particular, it is psychotherapy with children that highlights the play of masks as both showing and hiding. As initiated by Melanie Klein, playing in child psychotherapy tended at first to be more confined to the therapist's commentaries on the child's playing and the meaning of what the child did with the toys provided. Extended by Winnicott and others, the therapy increasingly took the form of mutual playing, where playing becomes interpretation. Alongside the unspoken, separate stream of meaning-making by patient and therapist, in work with children meaning is embedded not only in the activity of speech but in action—and, importantly, in acting out. Such activity reveals the interplay of free masks and forced masks and their link with the concept of projective identification.

The dust balls

A therapist, Peter Blake, writing in *Being Alive*, a collection of tributes to the work of Anne Alvarez, reports his difficulty in reaching an aggressive, contemptuous eight-year-old boy, Steven, who began to fling a ball of plasticine attached to a ball of string on to a high ledge . . . and pull the ball and inspect the dust that had collected on it . . . I entered the play, speaking as a piece of dust. In a rather high pitched voice I spoke about being dislodged from my home, that I wanted to stay with the rest of my dust family. [Blake, 2001, p. 81]

Blake comments that Steven began to listen properly, without contempt. In a newly childlike fashion, the boy kept asking what the dust was saying next, while the therapist, by playing the role of the dust, was astonished to find himself beginning to speak about being "only a speck of dust, so small, so worthless and so unwanted". From the new perspective of his assumed character—speck of dust—Blake began to realize "how much vulnerability and pain lay hidden behind Steven's hard, superior self" (*Ibid.*, p. 86). Via the role play, he more effectively identified with Steven's state.

It is, further, significant that Steven's game with the plasticine mimics so closely Freud's "Fort Da" game with the cotton reel, at the early stage of symbolic development (Freud, 1920g, p. 15) as discussed in Chapter Four. The eight-year-old Steven was perhaps alerting his therapist to the level of his early deprivation.

Such playing is one kind of beneficial protective mask that has an important intermediary or transitional function between subject and object, especially for vulnerable autistic and abused individuals. If the therapist tries directly to tackle their defences, for them it is like a pulverising of their very self. In protecting the child/self from direct exposure, this playing together is a vital route to the discovery of meaning and of meaning-making. Blake's experiencing himself as "only a speck of dust so small, so worthless and so unwanted" and his realization of the distress behind the mask of Steven's "hard, superior self" is a graphic illustration of the concept of projective identification. The withholding boy needed his therapist to know his hidden feelings, but could not communicate them directly to him.

With instinctive imagination, in taking on the role of the dust, Blake took on—introjected—as a "free" mask, the despised part of Steven—Steven's "forced" mask. This forced mask the child had split off and transferred to—projected into—the dust balls. Blake outlines the immense technical benefits of this shared enactment in its achieving an optimum mixture of closeness and distance between patient and therapist. The equivalent of—or substitute for—"interpretations" is mediated via the "mask" of the role play. But he also warns against retreats into the "dangerous safety of play" as a sort of collusive cosiness.

And if the potentially "dangerous safety of play" must be avoided, what about the potential danger of playing, in the form of violent acting out?

"All acting out is a breakdown in communication", declares Winnicott's celebrated colleague, Barbara Docker-Drysdale. In defining the necessary approach with violently disturbed and fragmented children, Drysdale's aim is the transformation of raw feelings into words: "To contain our feelings by transposing them into the symbols we call words" (Docker-Drysdale, 1991, p. 132). For this, the prime necessity with fragmented children, is to "hold the violence and the child together".

CHAPTER ELEVEN

The search for free masks

"The mirror would do well to reflect a little more before returning our image to us"

(Lacan, 1954, p. 138)

I n the following poem, the fundamental privacy of an imagined innermost self must be hidden by impregnable defences: the free masks of "a living double of you", a "two-fold guarded being" in the alternative translation, who is presented as robust rather than divided.

ADVICE

Ring with high walls the who you dream yourself.
After that, where the garden's visible
Through the wrought iron gate's affable grille,
Plant all the most smiling kinds of flowers,
That only so may people know you at all.
Where no-one's going to see it, plant nil.

Fix flower-beds like the neighbours have,
In which anyone peering may make out

Your garden as you mean them to descry it.
But where you're yours, and nobody ever sees it,
Let such flowers as come from the soil sprout,
Leave the natural herbs free to run riot.
Fix a living double of you, guard it
And make sure no-one who comes there and gazes
Can know more than a garden of who you be—
A showy, at the same time private, garden
Behind which the native flower grazes,
The herb so poor that even you don't see.

[Fernando Pessoa, 1935, p. 156]

The garden in the poem is an elaborate false trail. Unsuspecting peepers and spies must be fobbed off with convincingly beautiful shows that distract from the unassuming *"native flower"*, which *"grazes, / the herb so poor that even you don't see"*. So you become a living double of you, (or *"a two-fold guarded being"*—alternative translation of *faze de ti um duplo ser guardado*)[1] enabled safely and freely to *represent* your self and protect its hidden seeds.

In similar vein, Winnicott pictures a fortress self, guarded by defences that, far from being merely accretions, are integral to the personality, where the breaching of such defences would be unimaginably appalling. For him, too, the innermost self is always masked and naked selves cannot, must not, meet or directly communicate in words:

> I suggest that in health there is a core to the personality that corre-sponds to the true self of the split personality; I suggest that this core never communicates with the world of perceived objects, and that the individual person knows that it must never be communi-cated with or be influenced by external reality . . . *Each individual is an isolate, permanently non-communicating, permanently unknown, in fact, unfound* . . . Rape, and being eaten by cannibals, these are mere bagatelles as compared with the violation of the self's core, the alteration of the self's central elements by communication seeping through the defences. [Winnicott, 1965, p. 187]

In this imagined structure of the personality, there is no such thing as a self without its defences, its masks. So integral are these that it is valid to speak of "many selves" or "myself and many selves". For the being who is conjured up by Pessoa and Winnicott will appear not fixed at all, but fluid, mobile, subject to terrible distortions by pressures from within and without. It may sometimes feel as if these very defences of the innermost self are indeed breached. Far from appearing freely as *a two-fold guarded being*, or as *a living double of themselves* many people arrive for psychotherapy stuck with their forced Marcel Marceau (Chapter Nine) grinning masks of "compliance".

The therapist may then encourage, or be encouraged by, the patient to feel that the task is to get rid of, or strip off this grinning mask of compliance in order to reveal the patient's "True Self" or "child self". This is a doomed quest, since it often transpires that the naked "babe" that emerges, once the grin is effaced, is no more than another forced mask. And this mask is still more adept at fooling both therapist and patient that this new spontaneous creature is the "real thing". For what patients may begin by identifying as their vulnerable "true self", turns out, in the therapeutic process, to be an interloper, a shrivelled travesty of some archetypal creature, already far too naked and "found", too exposed to the eyes of imagined persecutors.

In order to become loosened from the grip of such an "infant", the patient needs to develop a free mask. This is the "second skin", or "psychic skin", corresponding to the original developmental point when, according to Winnicott, "there comes into existence what might be called a limiting membrane, which to some extent [in health] is equated with the surface of the skin, and has a position between the infant's "me" and his "not me" (Winnicott, 1965, p. 45). In the case of such patients, this distinction between me-and-not-me, between self and other, has either never quite taken place, or, through trauma, the psychic "skin" has broken. The skin, which acts as both bridge and boundary, is a way of describing the essential protective mask for communication between self and other.

Lily—the ventriloquist

My father groaned, my mother wept.
Into the dangerous world I leapt.

Helpless, naked, piping loud
Like a fiend hid in a cloud.

[William Blake]

In the case of Lily, a gifted fashion-designer, it felt as though her inner-most self was being worn on the outside, like a stigma for all to see. At first she experienced such distress in the simple act of entering the room, taking off her coat and arranging herself in the chair, all in front of the therapist, that she asked him not to come into the room until after she had settled herself. What appeared as her naked self seemed to be flip-side up. She had become totally identified with this self, in disso-ciation from more robust features of her personality. Yet because it felt so infantile and exposed, there was the feeling that this manifestation must be the "truest" part of her, with no distinction between the "baby" and the rest of her.

Thus, it was left to the therapist to hold a fuller vision of what might constitute the patient's personality than was yet available to the patient. It then helped to see this *illusion of* Lily's naked self rather as one of several forced masks that were wearing her. It also helped that the therapist did not agree to stay outside the room while Lily prepared to present or *re*-present herself.

Part of the therapeutic work then became the identification and naming of this usurping and diminished version of Lily's self that was stand-ing in for the whole. At first, both Lily and the therapist were taken in, tricked, by the needs and greeds of this "baby", seeing it/him/her as a pure expression of some primal, innocent self. But gradually, this view of Lily gave way to the recognition of a more malign baby ruling the roost, shaming and making its "mother"/patient feel such inappropri-ate and wretched nakedness in the presence of others.

This shift in perception was clinched when, one day, Lily recalled in some embarrassment an incident at a school reunion after her return from a long absence abroad. Surrounded by a group of old classmates congratulating her on her adventures, Lily became possessed by the voice of a young child, replying to her friends in a high-pitched squeak, "Oh yes, I have been to lots of places", and then flushing crimson, not knowing where to hide, to the obvious bewilderment of her compan-ions. This memory in the therapy session of having been suddenly possessed by a distinct and alien infant voice opened Lily's eyes to the possibility of a potential space between Her and It. Now there might be other aspects of her personality, other ways of being, that could be found and fostered.

Of further interest in this incident is that here it was the *voice* that acted as a forced mask. In the following illustration, it is primarily the *face* that is the vehicle first of forced masks and finally of free masks.

William—the mask maker

William's life was dominated by his mother's depression. He felt unmirrored, unheard, invisible. Speaking in a flat and toneless way, in the first session he rubbed his ear so constantly that it blazed, a crimson beacon, advertising William's need to be heard. His plight was that on the one hand he spoke of feeling himself to be the slave of successive forced masks, all of which wore him, but did not represent him or seem to belong to him. And on the other hand, on the most unsuitable occasions, what had slowly emerged as his supposedly real, little boy self, would erupt. For example, he would find himself raging or sulking with his boss and other authority figures. It became clear that, in one sense, this supposedly "authentic" child part was yet another forced mask and William's need became articulated in the therapy as the quest for free masks.

In work or social situations, assuming himself to be unnoticed, he would either subside into a poorly disguised sulk, or else explode in an embarrassing childish rage. This hurt, sometimes explosive "little boy", far from being a manifestation of William's child/true self, was a further forced mask. To compound the variations, if ever, on rare occasions, William imagined he was quite enjoying himself, someone was still bound to say, "What's wrong? What's up with you?" and, happening to glance in the pub mirror, William would be startled to see a tense, grim face staring back at him.

Such forced masks that, like Marcel Marceau's tortured grin, control the wearer, contrast with his lost, free, childhood clowning—which could also have been a defence, but at least the wearer was behind it. Thus, William's mask of "invisibility" was wounding; the hurt, sulky little boy had no suitable outer vesture; and the stony mask in the mirror was both alienating and misleading, epitomizing the gulf between his own perception of himself and the world's perception.

Things began to change when a literal mask came into play. William made a mask of himself in his sculpture class by lying down and placing over his face a layer of cling-film covered with strips of linen soaked in plaster of Paris. Although this immobilized him and prevented him from joining in the class chatter, he no longer felt excluded. The mask of himself protected and freed him. He felt part of the group, with a sense of great ease and satisfaction.

Not long after this, lying on the therapy couch in a state of deep depression about himself and the grey, sunless winter, William suddenly noticed that the position of two pictures in the room had been changed. He expressed perturbation and then said, in petulant, childish tones, "I want a picture on the *ceiling*. No, I want a *mirror* there." Then his attention was caught by the hitherto unnoticed light shade above his head and he asked if this was for a reading light. "I want more light," he demanded. The therapist responded, "Why not switch it on?" "I can't reach," he said, nevertheless reaching up from his prone position and switching it on. But after a moment, he complained, "It's far too light!" and put out the light. It seemed as though the experience in the sculpture class was linked with this first direct appearance in the room with the therapist of the enforced, sulky little-boy mask, pointing therefore to William's potential liberation from this mask.

As for the forced stony mask, William was passionately recalling favourite childhood haunts, from which, as the therapist pointed out, his mother and father seemed notable by their absence. "Oh, not at all!" said William. "Mum was always there and I used to hang around her all the time, trying to protect her!"

"Protect her?" repeated the therapist. "From what?"

"Oh, there were two nasty girls who taunted her for being a witch."

Startled by this disclosure, the therapist asked why this might have been and how William recalled his mother at this time. "Well," he replied, "She looked very like me. The same grim, stony face and dark hair and the same hooked nose—only more so."

"So," suggested the therapist, "the only way of shielding your mother from the two bad girls was to take away her mask and wear it yourself."

Instead of dismissing this as fanciful, William became tearful and replied that from that time his mother had indeed become more lively. But this he had always attributed to thyroid pills given by the doctor. "So," the therapist concluded, "your mother went to the doctor and you came to therapy."

The case of William, in its mixture of concreteness and metaphor (treated more fully in Richards, 1994, pp. 35–47), points to how a patient's masks, conscious and unconscious, serve as signposts towards not some unitary truth of the personality, but towards a fuller grasp of its manifold nature.

The example, in William's case, of a literal mask of his face highlights the naked face itself as a primary mask. It specifically raises the question of how far is it possible to be in charge of the masks of one's unmasked face, to 'Fix a living double of you'? And when might it be right for the therapist to point out these forced facial masks, as when the therapist asked his patient, "Why are you smiling then?" during her lamentation of Diana's death (Chapter Five)?

The absolute vulnerability and fragility of the face for the philosopher Levinas, in expressing the inescapability of reflecting and being reflected by others, underlines the precariousness of the task of the face as vehicle of many masks:

> The proximity of the other is the face's meaning, and it *means* from the very start in a way that goes beyond those plastic forms which forever try to cover the face like a mask of their presence to perception. But always the face shows through these forms. Prior to any particular expression and beneath all particular expressions, which cover over and protect with an immediately adopted face or countenance, there is the nakedness and destitution of the expression as such, that is to say extreme exposure, defencelessness, vulnerability itself. [Levinas, 1993 p. 82]

But forced masks and free masks are not solely concerned with vulnerability. For the notion of many masks as integral to the personality enables a questioning of the frequent equation of self with all that is true, noble and genuine, accompanied by a disavowal of any defects of character as "false", as "not really me", "not myself today", etc.—a form of dissociation voiced by both "normal" and psychopathic people. As queried by the Kleinian analyst, Clifford Scott, "What about the *evil* True Self?" (Milner, 1952, p. 82). For the person who either is seen as "evil" or who is saddled with the conviction of his/her own essential badness, the concept of varied masks can mitigate such simplistic labelling. Masks assist both patient and therapist in reaching disowned or unconscious aspects of the personality and crippling misidentifications.

One psychoanalytical approach to this question of evil visualized by the post-Kleinian Donald Meltzer in his allegory *The*

Claustrum (Meltzer, 1992) intriguingly construes adverse aspects of the personality and their potential transformation by imagining what could be regarded as a range of forced masks. The Claustrum is the infant's/individual's phantasied internal mother's interior, where "intruders" get stuck to bad parts in bad spaces. According to Meltzer, such a conceit has the potential for a new approach to the theory and phenomenon of human depravity. He claims that it becomes possible to "eliminate evil as an intrinsic concept and reduce it to a behavioural, descriptive one" (*ibid.*, p. 92).

Meltzer builds on the idea that intrusive projective identification of lost parts of the self, especially the "child", or "True Self" into the bad objects of the Claustrum enables the analyst to visualize a more rounded human being in the patient than the "alien" lounging on his couch. This may be saying more about Meltzer than the patient, but potentially the conceit allows the analyst to picture a redeemable and reachable bad enmeshed part of the self.

If this potential for transformation is held in mind by another (i.e., therapist), the enmeshed self may be prised or coaxed apart from the bad object, this rectal space of the internal mother's body, which is the source of poison. Such a fanciful vision, if it carries any clout, could imply for psychoanalytic practice a far more significant role in human affairs. It could, indeed, be world shaking if, in Meltzer's words, "this great malignant object is potentially metabolisable into its component parts of self and object, dissolving the malignant character of the combination" (*ibid.*, pp. 92–93). Moreover, to evil are assigned solely human, rather than meta-physical dimensions, so that "evil"—and other traits of Claustrum dwellers—can be seen as one among a range of forced masks, with the potential for metamorphosis into free masks.

The metaphors of acquiring Masks and of "growing" a "second" or "psychic skin" as ways of describing essential defences of the personality gain a fresh perspective from the celebrated actor of Beckett's works, Billie Whitelaw. Whitelaw testifies to an awesome reversal of this process of masking, both in performance and in her own life.

Whitelaw played the woman in *Not I*, who could not say "I" or "me", but only "*Not I*", until the very last words of the play. Throughout, she was immobilized, strapped in a chair, the stage in total darkness, apart from her bell-clapping tongue and wide-open mouth. Before each performance, Whitelaw would instruct herself, "Let your skin fall off. Let your flesh and bones fall off. Leave only the *centre*". At the end of each performance, she was so drained that she had to be carried off the stage.

Also, when her five-year-old son with raging meningitis was given a maximum of three days to live, Whitelaw banished every-one, stripped to the waist and from this bare "centre" of herself, clasped the dying child for three days and nights. His survival was seen as miraculous, but, for Whitelaw, it was natural: the life from her very centre had been coursing into him: "My centre flowed from me to him".

So—masks and defences: yes. But their potential shedding: yes and yes!

Note

1.   ADVICE

    Surround with high walls whoever you dream you are.
    Then, where the garden can be seen
    Through the gate with its bestowing bars,
    Place whatever flowers are most smiling,
    So they may know you only like that.
    Where no one will see it, plant nothing.
    Make flowerbeds like the ones other people have
    Where glances may glimpse your garden,
    Such as you are going to show it to them.
    But where you are yours and it is seen by no one,
    Let the flowers that come from the garden grow
    And let the natural grasses flourish.
    Make of yourself a two-fold guarded being;
    And may no one who might see or watch
    Know more of who you are than a garden-
    A garden conspicuous and set-apart,
    Behind which the native flower brushes
    Grass so poor that not even you can see it.

[Fernando Pessoa, 1935]

(alternative translation by J. Greene and
C. De Azevedo Mafra)

PART THREE

SIGNS AND TIMES

"ON THE STAGE, IT IS ALWAYS NOW"

> . . . anything can happen, everything is possible and proba-
> ble. Time and space do not exist. On a light groundwork
> of reality, imagination spins and weaves new patterns
> made up of memories, experiences, unfettered fancies and
> improvisations.
>
> (Strindberg, 1955, pp. 269–270)

Patient: For the first time I feel that I am here myself. That means
that I was unaware of time at the end of the last session. I got
carried away.

Analyst: Your true self has its own time, in contrast to your false
self which keeps in touch with clocks. [Winnicott, 1986, p. 125]

CHAPTER TWELVE

Time, fantasy, and imagination

The now doesn't exclude the past because the past shapes and animates the present. The past is alive in the present without being alive *as* the past, alive in explicit memory—just as a violinist's phrasing flows from her practice sessions without her needing to have any explicit memory of them. I believe that shaping is what matters most; this is the deepest continuance of memory ... [Strawson, 04.01.03.]

Imagine a child putting its hand in a flame. The bodily sensation of pain teaches the brain about danger. "I will not touch fire again or it will hurt", thinks the child. But when the child learns this lesson, it is imagining a being that does not yet exist: its own future self.

So "the brain is mapping a body that is still only imaginary. From [physical] feeling comes the capacity for imagination and hence for empathy. If we can imagine our future self, we can also imagine other selves". [Bate, 2003]

These observations offer a sense of how being-in-the-world is constrained by the dialectic between present, past and future. "Where" we are in relation to both inner and actual time is a measure of psychic well-being. The absolute supremacy and dominion of the present is, paradoxically, wholly dependent on its shaping by the past, on imagining the future and the possible consequences of the present.

In Good Time, therefore, *"the past is alive in the present without being alive as the past"*, and we "can imagine our future self, and . . . also imagine other selves". But when the past is alive in the present *and also alive as the past*, with the usurping of imagination by fantasy, this points to disturbance in time—Bad Time or Time Sickness.

The necessity of giving the "time factor" its full weight is an important theme in the work of Winnicott. He refers to what can be a catastrophic interference with the infant's unfolding in time and space, and with those essential long periods of secure unintegration, the slipping into bits and pieces in sleep and rest, alternating with phases of integration, when "from time to time, the infant comes together and feels something" (Winnicott, 1958, p. 150). It is Winnicott's sensitivity to the most delicate and subtle shifts in internal states, as well as to the floridly anguished, that alerts him to the significance of disturbed continuity. In his concern to stress the infant's vulnerability, Winnicott attempts to formulate, with algebraic precision, the adverse consequences of maternal delay in responding to its cries:

> In $x+y+z$ minutes, the baby has become traumatised. In $x+y+z$ minutes the mother's return does not mend the baby's altered state. Trauma implies that the baby has experienced a break in life's continuity, so primitive defences now become organised to defend against a repetition of 'unthinkable anxiety' or a return of the acute confusional state that belongs to disintegration of nascent ego structure. [Winnicott, 1971, p. 97]

In Winnicott's remarkable study, "Dreaming, fantasying and living" (Winnicott, 1971, p. 26ff), the woman patient portrayed is alienated from herself and therefore cannot be fully here or fully now. Mostly, she floats "outside" time in what she calls a "fantasying" state. Winnicott speaks of the "time factor" that "is operative" and which "is different according to whether the patient is *fantasying* or *imagining*. In the fantasying, what happens, happens immediately, except that it does not happen at all" (*ibid.*, p. 27). The patient "longs to find something that will make her do things, to use every waking minute, to be able to say, 'It is now and not tomorrow, tomorrow'" (*ibid.*, p. 32). But since "fantasying paralyses action" (*ibid.*, p. 33), she cannot constructively plan for tomorrow, nor look forward to real action.

To be able to picture the past and imagine the future in such a dynamic way depends on a firm foothold in the present, allowing continuity of being and a full embodiment in time and space. The imagination is freed for creative playing and meaning-making, sparking off spontaneous ideas and communications. The thought seems to precede the thinker as in the free association of psychotherapy illustrated in the sequence involving "dementors", "demons" and "daemons" (Chapter Six). The players are wholly *there*, living each moment fully.

What Winnicott wants for his patient is for her imagination to take over from her fantasying. For imagining belongs to the essential self, the depths of her personality, signalling wholeness and creativity. Any stirrings of her imagination, allow her to be fully here in the present rather than fantasying from a distant, dissociated part of herself. Whenever in a session she is in a more imaginative inte-grated state, she can also make links and think symbolically and—of vital importance—while asleep she can dream. She becomes more able to "constructively plan for tomorrow, and look forward to real action" (*ibid.*, p. 33).

Elsewhere, Winnicott connects fantasy with schoolboy-type adventure stories and grandiose, "Walter Mitty"-type day-dreaming. It appears as part of the manic defence associated with flights from the inner world of the self (Winnicott, 1958, p. 129). However, when his fantasying patient brings a night-time dream, coming from her very centre or core, he sees that this has put her in touch with live feelings and creative playing.

Unlike Winnicott's fantasying patient, rather than drifting *outside* time, others who are time-disturbed may colonize a particu-lar segment of time, giving it unnatural prominence and so interrupt the natural flow of past, present, and future. Unlike Winnicott's drifting patient, fantasy in these positions is often highly purposeful and focused, while also undermining and unrealistic.

For Winnicott, therefore, fantasy appears defensive rather than creative. It is opposed to imagination. Fantasy resembles and is illu-minated by the poet Coleridge's contrasting of what he refers to as the cerebral activity of *fancy* with *imagination*. The hallmark of fancy for Coleridge is the yoking together or equating of ideas and images which at first sight appear effective and true, but which are ultimately hollow, unsatisfying, without depth or resonance. Fancy sprouts similes, which may appear contrived, rather than metaphors, which reveal the subject in a newer, truer light.

For example, a comparison between two illustrations from the work of the Metaphysical poet, John Donne, clarifies this possible contrast between *imagination* and *fancy*.

In the first, from "A Valediction: Forbidding Mourning", the following lines crown a lover's careful breaking to his mistress that he is about to leave her. He argues that it will not be a real separation because their "two soules are one", concluding with the following analogy between their twin souls and a pair of compasses:

> If they be two, they are two so
> As stiffe twin compasses are two,
> Thy soule the fixt foot, makes no show
> To move, but doth if th'other doe.
>
> And though it in the centre sit,
> Yet when the other far doth rome,
> It leans and hearkens after it,
> And grows erect, as that comes home.
>
> Such wilt thou be to mee, who must
> Like th'other foot, obliquely runne;
> Thy firmness makes my circle just,
> And makes me end where I begunne.
>
> [Donne, 1980, p. 84]

Looking at this specious or special pleading in terms of the poet's adopted persona of a departing lover, is this an inspired and apt metaphor of true closeness, likely to touch and convince his mistress? Or might it not rather be experienced by her as a contrived and *fanciful* conceit, a discernible split in the lover between head and heart.

Compare those lines with Donne, as the reneging "lover"/ sinner, in a passionate appeal to his God. This is an urgent imperative, where the argument organically unfolds, in a total fusion of the literal and metaphoric, a powerful evocation of divine pressure upon his errant soul. The words of this sonnet belong to imaginative fullness, to a unified sensibility with no discernible ironic gap between "head" and "heart".

> Batter my heart, three person'd God; for, you
> As yet but knocke, breathe, shine and seek to mende;
> That I may rise, and stand, o'erthrow me and bend
> Your force, to break, blowe, burn and make me new.
> I, like an usurpt towne, to' another due,
> Labour to' admit you, but Oh, to no end,
> Reason your viceroy in me, me should defend,
> But is captiv'd, and proves weake or untrue.
> Yet dearly' I love you and would be loved faine,
> But am betrothed unto your enemie:
> Divorce mee,' untie, or breake that knot again;
> Take mee to you, imprison mee, for I
> Except you' enthrall mee, never shall be free,
> Nor ever chast, except you ravish mee.
>
> [*ibid.*, p. 314]

Applying the activity of fantasy or fancy to disrupted temporal relationships, conscious fantasies get falsely yoked to times, places, and experiences, which do not reflect today's reality. These compulsive attachments and obsessions may feel right and true to the person concerned. Possibly they have originated in imaginative vitality, but they slowly stiffen into split-off fantasy. In fantasying states, to a greater or lesser degree, people are out of their time and without strong roots in the present.

In *fantasy* one is likely to roam in the more purely speculative tenses, to turn these into "real time". These are the twilight tenses of "what *might have been*", "what *will have been*", "what *should have been*", "what *will* be", unleashing all kinds of fortune-telling, reading of tea leaves, and other inappropriate temporal meddlings.

Although highlighted in the acts apart of therapy and theatre, such temporal deviations are often unnoticed in the ordinary world, where certain moments, present and past, get similarly framed-off, in a surfeit of meaning. Whether good or bad, such moments become magnified, indelible, if from the past they leap out of the shadows to wreck a perfectly cordial encounter. Or, suddenly, unexpectedly, a moment, a sequence in the present flow of experience gets isolated, cut off, as if you are trapped in a cave, rather than borne along by the tide. These are strong manifestations of the past "*being alive* as *the past*".

The study, in Chapter Thirteen, of the staging of *Purgatory*, will focus primarily on how "on the stage it is always now", how all time phases are made present—*re-presented* by means of staging, props and above all, words. To the therapist with a similar function of rendering all things present, of re-presenting, I apply Heidegger's metaphor of man as the "shepherd of being". Chapter Thirteen sets the scene for the temporal variations viewed in the succeeding chapters.

"A dead, living murdered man!"

"The action takes place in a perpetual present ... On the
stage it is always now." In other words, "the passage of time
in the drama is an absolute succession of presents".

(Wilder, quoted in Elam, 1980, p. 117)

Purgatory by W. B. Yeats (1938)

Yeats's poetic and profoundly oedipal drama, *Purgatory* is an
extreme theatrical illustration of the maxim, "On the stage,
it is always now" (p. 219). The "it" in the statement, "On the
stage it is always now" refers not solely to the immediacy of a stage
performance, but extends to encompass past, future, and fantasy
times. Not only what *will* be, but also what might be and what
might have been, all equally become "now"—and therefore "real".
(*ibid.*). Such simultaneity of tenses levels all personal time in
theatre, as in therapy. It contrasts with the early Freudian kind of
"excavation", and Sherlock Holmes' clue-hunting of the past.

Purgatory brings off the feat of making present, of "re-present-ing", simultaneously with the present of the play, events from even before the conception of the two initially alive protagonists: an Old Man and his sixteen-year-old son. Thanks to the central conceit of the play, both become witnesses to the original parental coupling between the Old Man's father and mother, who are thus the *grand-parents* of the young boy.

This central conceit is that the sinning mother/grandmother is condemned to the Purgatory of repeatedly reliving, on each anniversary of its performance, her original degrading sexual act with her drunken gamekeeper husband, which had resulted in the Old Man's conception. According to the Old Man, only if someone intervenes to break this cycle and puts an end to the mother's penance, will her perpetual *redreaming* of her offence come to an end.

The Old Man, having himself knifed his mother's husband—his own despised father— fifty years ago, is still welded to and tormented by the fantasy that each repetition of the ghostly sexual act nevertheless involves, for his dead mother, a renewal of sexual pleasure. His further fantasy is that the one means of ending this cycle is to slay his own sixteen-year-old son with the same knife.

This time-sick fantasy falsely yokes the distant past and the unborn future to here and now, giving them a bogus equality with the present.

But before sacrificing his son, the Old Man insists that the boy also witness the *re-presented* primal scene on this, its anniversary.

Thematically, this brief poetic drama is an embodiment of Time-Sickness in an extreme perversion of tenses. *What has been* becomes falsely identified with *what will be*. Diseased fantasy displaces dreaming and imagination in the central character: the Old Man, with his adhesion to the sins, figures and deeds of the past and to the "dreaming" of his dead mother.

The re-presenting on stage of these long past events into the present of the participants is apparently a literal, visible re-enactment of what can come to pass metaphorically in psychotherapy. In therapy, the images that arise are conjured up mainly by words. But, actually, the fate of images arising in both theatre and therapy depends on the perception of the participants and their treatment of such images. As mentioned in Chapter One, the present makes the past, as much as the past shapes the present. The text of the play is therefore a precursor of the clinical material that follows. And my chief purpose is to draw on parallels between the magnetism of *nowness* on the stage achieved by the range of theatrical devices and nowness in therapy, with the person of the therapist as its facilitator.

The setting of *Purgatory* is *a ruined house and a bare tree in the back-ground*. This tree is pointed out by the Old Man to his sixteen-year-old son (and, importantly, to the audience) as *stripped bare*, in contrast to the time, fifty years ago, "*Before the thunderbolt had riven it*", when he had beheld this tree with "*Green leaves, ripe leaves, leaves as thick as butter, / Fat, greasy life*".

This evocation of the tree's former fruitfulness contends with its now visible-on-the-stage bareness and prepares for the eerie illumination of the ruined house. Past and present are compressed into the present-ness of the single tree image .

The Old man commands the boy, "*. . . Stand there and look, / Because there's somebody in that house*". The boy, at first, sees only a derelict ruin, but the Old Man insists that a figure is visible and has returned to the scene of her former sins, in order to "*Relive [her] transgressions not once but many times.*".

Now occurs the direct enactment of the play's central conceit, the Old Man's fantasy that, through *dream*, past transgressions must be repeated until *that consequence is at an end*. The Old Man cries,

> Listen to the hoof-beats! Listen! Listen! . . .
>   Beat! Beat!
> This night is the anniversary
> Of my mother's wedding night,
> Or of the night wherein I was begotten.
> My father is riding from the public-house,
> A whiskey bottle under his arm.

> [p. 223]

Then, suddenly, according to the stage directions:

> (*A window is lit showing a young girl.*)

She is quite visible to the audience, though not yet to the boy. The Old Man comments on his father's arrival at the young girl's (i.e., his own mother's) bedchamber. So now both we, the audience, and the Old Man are directly observing the moment immediately prior to the Old Man's own conception.

Then he, who at this multiple moment is simultaneously both an old man and an as yet unbegotten infant, cries out to his long-dead, young-girl mother, begging her to resist yet another repetition of the on-scene "ob-scene" sexual act:

> Old Man: "The window is dimly lit again.
> Do not let him touch you! It is not true
> That drunken men cannot beget,
> And if he touch he must beget
> And you must bear his murderer".

[pp. 223–224]

It is as if the Old Man, in seeking to prevent his own original conception, desires to wipe out his total existence.

Then the boy also sees the *lit-up* window, showing *a man pouring whiskey into a glass.*

> Boy: "My God! The window is lit up
> And somebody stands there, although
> The floorboards are all burnt away."

[p. 225]

This vision is both objectively there, as also witnessed by the audience, but equally, it is the Old Man who opens the boy's eyes and makes past present. In bemused shock, at the vision of his slain grandfather-to-be, the boy cries,

> "A dead, living murdered man!"

[p. 225]

So now, in addition to the Old Man, the future/present grandchild of this long past, again to be consummated union, becomes witness to the original event, horrified at

> "A body that was a bundle of old bones
> Before I was born. Horrible! Horrible!"
> *[he covers his eyes]*

[p. 225]

The audience now witness a struggle between the Old Man and his son over the former's money-bag and the Old Man suddenly turns on the boy, slaying him with that same knife originally used to kill his own father.

[*He stabs and stabs again. The window grows dark*] Once more; the Old Man sings a lullaby to his dead "living" mother. And now *the stage has grown dark,* but, as well as the re-presented window, *the tree, stands in white light* and the Old Man celebrates his mother's presumed deliverance from Purgatory, thanks to his murder of her grandson, his son (p. 226).

But his rejoicing proves premature for, once again, he hears the sound of ghostly hoof-beats signalling the next renewal of the sexual encounter. He realizes that neither his own intervention in slaying the Boy, nor his mother's own mind *can hold up that dream.* For he himself is *twice a murderer and all for nothing* (p. 226).

But in the closing moments, we detect a shift in the Old Man's perception from sick fantasying welded to the ghost of his mother towards a more imaginative stance. His omnipotence and omniscience shattered, the Old Man finally puts himself and his imprisoning fantasy, falsely perceived as his mother's *dream,* into the hands of God, pleading

"O God,
Release my mother's soul from its dream!
Mankind can do no more."

[p. 227]

The temporal gymnastics of *Purgatory,* the enactment in the play's *present* of a long past deed, the simultaneity of past and present tenses, highlight the panoply of potential devices behind the usually dominant instrument of the spoken word.

These devices or codes are in play in both theatre and therapy. In *Purgatory* they include verbal references, the imagery and visual treatment, through the lighting of the set, through the props and unifying images—especially the house, the tree, and the knife, and the contribution of sound effects—though note that sound of the fateful hoof-beats, are heard only in the audience's imagination through the Old Man's words. Thanks to these devices, coupled with the central conceit of ritual, ghostly repetition of an ancient act, the past is not merely evoked, but rendered coterminus with, simultaneous with, the present, an extreme fulfilment of the dictum, "On the stage it is always now." All times are sucked into the vortex of this present.

The shepherd of being (Heidegger)

Similarly, on the analytic stage, the extreme gravitational pull of the present ensures that the *present makes* the past, as much as ever the past made the present, and perhaps almost as much as the present makes the future. As explained by George Steiner, for the phenomenological philosopher, Heidegger, "Being is being in the world. There is nowhere else . . . Being and authenticity can only be realised *within immanent existence and time* (Steiner, 1978, p. 64, italics added).

Not only is there "no-*where* else", but also there is "no-*when*-else". Neither past nor future exist from our inescapable standpoint of "now", despite the many imaginative and ingenious ways of seeming to bring them forth and make them real. For as already suggested, it is fantasy and the speculative tenses that strive in vain towards the obsolete or premature materialization of other times. (The findings of quantum mechanics, "The Theory of Everything", have not yet produced a real-life time-traveller.) And even what constitutes the yoke of "now" is threaded with nothing more solid than drops of dew, ceaselessly evaporating, never to be grasped.

It is this inescapability of being-in-the-world that may have prompted Heidegger's metaphor of mankind as the "shepherd of being" (Steiner, 1978, p. 63). This image can be applied in a very specific way to the psychotherapist, when working with those whose relationships to time are disturbed. The patient gets wedged into split-off time segments by inappropriate fantasies. And continuity of being is broken. To be thus torn in time is to be a divided self. To hide mentally in any one temporal position means being at best only half here now; or, as in early infancy, so excessively here now, that there can be no link with past or future; or else seemingly lost *outside* time, like Winnicott's fantasying patient (Chapter Twelve).

In the insistent pull of the present on the analytic stage, the therapist is the vessel through which all other times are poured. The inexorability of this present, as the fifty-minute hour trickles or roars by, is one source of potential health, of healing for those time-scarred, "time-saturated" people (Heidegger, 1980, p. 83), washed up on the shores of psychotherapy. What, then, is on offer from the therapist, the shepherd of being, is a turn-around in these jumbled and disturbed relationships to time. Faced with the uncompromising here-and-nowness of the therapy and the person of the therapist, these refugees are shown the natural unfolding of time: the foregrounded present, flanked discreetly by the past as past and the future as future. Those who "don't know how to be" now and here can discover, with the therapist, a centring in the present, with the possibility of continuity, of links between times, facilitating a more cordial co-existence between the self's disparate aspects.

CHAPTER FOURTEEN

This year

I n this and ensuing chapters, I am loosely distinguishing between states of disturbance in Time by the labels of "This year", "Next year", "Sometime" (including "Last year"), and "Never". Each position is marked by difficulty in the fundamental linking up of past, present, and future, in making connections that allow one to be firmly held in the time process and in surrendering to the flow of time. Any of these artificially labelled states is accompanied by a considerable shake-up and shuffling of tenses, as if there is *no-when* and *nowhere* to rest one's head.

In contrast to the healthy location in a present securely linked to the concept of past and future, to time's natural unfolding, "This year" refers to the shadow side of presentness, to states when the patient may seem to be so imprisoned in single, cut-off moments that the temporal chain is snapped. Nothing is real in the patient's mind but his/her perception of the therapist's moment-to-moment behaviour and the patient's immediate feelings. Each moment becomes a separate framed-off act apart. Therapist and patient are trapped inside a space capsule, where, instead of links with the past and possible future, there is only a surrounding darkness.

"This year" fantasies are often marked by the eruption of two or more dominant inner figures—or "forced masks" (Chapter Eleven)—in deadly warfare with each other. These figures or forced masks might include a clamorous, insatiable baby, some version of a harsh witch, plus "whoever" it is that is responsible for the patient's turning up for his/her therapy session. This "whoever" is felt to be a helpless witness to the "others" in their struggle.

Behind this manifest struggle is often the "unconscious wish magically to turn the clock back and be a baby, with the analyst as an ideal infancy mother" (Ledermann, 1989, p. 108). But such a wish simultaneously arouses the saboteur/witch's insistence that any food from the therapist is poisonous and must be resisted. The therapist must contend with the patient's urge to resist and wreck each moment, to kill hope and the unborn future. In a "This year" state the patient feels utterly exposed and unmasked. Because the focus is on very bruised or fragile aspects of the self, the essential masks—the "twofold guard" or "living double of you" (Chapter Eleven), fail to function. In this state, where the therapist's words and meanings pierce and stab, either withdrawal or attack seem the only options. Meanings become so bloated as to be unbearable.

By this slicing off of the present from both past and future the patient is signalling that s/he feels utterly allergic to linking. For the linking involved in meaning-making *takes time*. An interpretation or a reflection or a question involves a linking, a relationship with what has gone before and with what will follow. Yet in a "This year" state, there is no ongoing time, only swollen moments. From this allergy to a surfeit of meaning-making, the individual needs to rest in a pre-symbolic, non-projective environment, "which is, in effect the mother, the mother and father, the place, affecting the baby before the era of control by projection and introjection (Winnicott, 1963, p. 480). For whether or not conscious memory is suspended in a "This year" state, *unconscious phantasy* and the unremembered past are active, as the account of Winnicott's "Friday Afternoon" will suggest.

"A complete disaster"

Any random or accidental alteration in the therapy room is not only highly significant. It can be devastating. In his paper entitled,

"Meeting regression in psychoanalysis", Winnicott graphically describes the "complete disaster" of his inadvertently altering an element in the setting provided for a very dependent patient. It is striking that this account sounds very like the setting of a stage scene before a performance begins:

> In regard to this patient there are certain things that have to be the same always. The curtains are drawn; the door is on the latch so that the patient can come straight in; all the arrangements in the room must be constant and also there are some objects which are variable but which belong to the transference relationship. At the time that I am describing the constant object is placed in a certain position on the desk and there are certain papers which have accumulated which I put beside me waiting for the moment when the patient will want them back.

> This Friday in spite of careful inspection of my arrangements I leave the papers on top of the other object instead of putting them beside me. The patient comes into the room and sees these alterations, and when I arrive on the scene I find that this is a complete disaster. I see at the moment of entering the room what has happened and I know that I shall be very lucky if we recover from this disaster in a matter of weeks. [Winnicott, 1989, p. 96]

Winnicott's tiny omission sparked off such a blaze, that "now" became all engulfing. While acknowledging the extremity of this patient's reaction to the disturbance of the setting, and going on to show how use in the session was gradually made of his "bad behaviour", Winnicott makes no attempt to diminish the magnitude of his action, but wholly endorses, colludes with [which literally means "plays with"], the patient's view and the communication implicit in her desperate reaction. He refers repeatedly to his "disastrous mistake". It is striking that he tells us also that he in fact abstained from interpretation himself, saying that, "Before the end of the hour in this case I was able to talk about the whole thing in the way that she asked me to do, which is rather different from giving an interpretation" (ibid.).

Although Winnicott makes the further point that the episode also gave rise to some new insights about the patient's past relationship to her father, it looks as if "the way that she asked" him to "talk about the whole thing" was that he should simply take it at its face value and focus on the magnitude of his offence. Although we don't fully get her side of the story, this surely has much to do with the implicit immensity of the patient's own inner, partly private, interpretative activity. In her absolute dependence on Winnicott's full understanding of all *her* needs and meanings, she attributes massive significance to this "proof" of his "failure" fully to grasp her state.

Thus everything tends to hinge on the opening moments of a session. If the therapist gets it "wrong", his/her words are already poisonous, so it is already "too late. No point. It's over". No hope of either "beating: the witch or of contacting her by detoxifying her. The witch becomes equated with—projected into—the therapist, who is now dangerous and must be avoided.

Putting the clock back

For Beth, who attacked the therapist's "text-book interpretations" (Chapter Five), while she too was trapped in the unbearable pressure of *this* moment, there was a shuffling up of tenses, with *now* irrevocably blighting the non-existent future. She was convinced that the bad happening now, in the session, had "already" doomed all future sessions. Feeling that there was no self inside her, because there was no "where" for such a self to be, Beth experienced movement through time and space and every kind of transition as threatening and dangerous. For her, rather than a flow of time, there were only transitions. Beth could not adjust from work to weekend, or to changes in routine or in seasons. She could not face the movement from one element to another—like swimming or air-travel.

The unbearable intensity of nowness was expressed in a desperate attempt to control clock time to pre-empt the otherwise dreaded future—and dread, according to Winnicott, is memory in the future (Winnicott, 1989, p. 87).

Beth found the transition from outside to inside the therapist's house agonizing. On arrival, she would manage a breathless "hallo" and, upstairs in the consulting room, would perch trembling, on the edge of her chair, facing away from the therapist—towards the window, where, at first, the clock was situated for the therapist to glance at unobtrusively. Never meeting his eyes, if he failed magically to unlock Beth's words, she considered that his own were already poisonous.

Despite the extension of the session to one and a half hours, if she was not immediately launched, it was already "too late. No point. It's over". No hope of either "beating" (Beth's word) the witch or of contacting her by detoxifying her.

Any sense of process was obliterated and, with that, all possibility of reparation. Like Lady Macbeth, Beth felt the "future i' the instant"; "what's done cannot be undone". So she knew now that she would be unable to come back "tomorrow and tomorrow and tomorrow." For the rest of the session, she would subside into a kind of blazing silence, when both Beth and her therapist were aware of the clock hands whizzing round at an alarming rate towards the inevitable, unresolved end.

One day, Beth explained that she could not bear to look at her own watch. Yet she couldn't see the therapist's clock in its place on the window sill. So she asked the therapist to move his clock to the table by his chair, in order that she herself would also be able to view the time. The therapist complied. Then, not long after this, Beth came bearing what seemed to be a cassette player, which she nervously placed on the bed beside her chair. It proved, however, to be a clock radio, brought because Beth found, after all, that she could not even *look towards* the clock in its new place right beside the therapist and facing Beth.

With the presence now of two clocks and two watches, during the ensuing witch-dominated silence, the therapist ventured to say, "All our four time-keepers agree that we still have half an hour to go, so how about it?" This intervention worked and Beth, with a reluctant laugh, somehow got wound up and ticking over. The clock radio made no more appearances. But soon afterwards, in an unusually communicative session, Beth suddenly halted, mid-sentence and plunged into a new, implacable silence, because, as she eventually confessed, she had seen the therapist glance at his watch while she was talking. The therapist reminded her that he could no longer unobtrusively look at, or see the clock, because of its new position facing away from him towards Beth.

"Couldn't you put it on the window sill facing you?" Beth demanded.

"You mean back in its original place?" queried the therapist.

"I forget!" she snapped. So he put the clock back . . . (cf. Richards, 1993, pp. 17–29).

CHAPTER FIFTEEN

. . . Next year . . .

A "Next year" state may be dominated by either of two scenarios, which are two sides of the same coin. One is the haunting vision of a dreaded future and the other, the vision of an urgently desired, "perfect" future, often hinges on demanding the immediate alteration of a single element in the present.

The dreaded future

This is marked by the belief that safety and satisfaction lie in the power to control time, in its not-yet-happened form: the future. Only if the patient has planned the session in advance and has studied the therapist's ways sufficiently to know how he will react, can she face coming to the session. There is an urgent need to make safe the unexploded future, which applies as much to the next minute as to next week and next year. The anxiety behind this is expressed by controlling, knowing, and being *ready* for any eventuality that the terrorist/therapist might drop on her. Control, now, of that future which does not exist, is the most pressing concern. One patient arrived for her session, saying, "I feel as if I've had the session already. I have been rehearsing what I wanted to tell you as I came across the fields. It's so much easier than actually being here now—I don't know what to say now. It's a pity we couldn't just communicate by telepathy . . ."

When the attempted control of what will happen breaks down, this is replaced by "knowledge"—the certainty, beforehand, of a bad outcome. The patient springs into "knowing" in advance what is going to happen, or what the therapist will do. For example, "I had this dream last night, but I know what you'll say about it, so I won't tell it." Or as a protection against the doomed future, the patient collects the precious insights gained in a session with the parting words, "Now how am I going to hang on to these to shield me from trouble?"

It is, nevertheless, surely vital that, rather than challenging such defences, the therapist understands their necessity as ways of managing the stress of therapy. This applies especially to the use of diaries. One apparent advantage for the diarist: the pain the patient feels while the bad experience is actually happening can be simultaneously converted in her mind into a narrative of the *past*, for the *future* witty entertainment of therapist, friends, or both, and for her own catharsis in writing and reading her own account. In order to survive the challenge of today, another patient turned it into an instant "yesterday" and "tomorrow", by writing a blow-by-blow commentary of her doings between sessions. This allowed her to control the future—the next session—by filling it with what she had written about the past, reading it aloud to the therapist.

Someone else, lamenting that she had no idea who she was, arrived with diaries going back to the age of twelve, and for three sessions she read them aloud, in increasing astonishment at their forgotten contents. This buffer helped her soon to feel sufficiently secure in the room with the therapist to abandon the diaries. She had instinctively exploited her past for the sake of controlling the future of the next session. Whatever time she was unable to shape or control in this way, this person resorted to "knowing". And here, dread of the future merges with desire. Desperately seeking a long-term partner, she consulted a fortune-teller, pinning all her faith on the promise that her "certain destiny is entwined with a man who awaits her".

The desired future

For the fantasy "perfect future" to be realized, the therapist is expected to cooperate actively. Unlike Winnicott's drifting patient (cf. Chapter Twelve), the "Next year" patient can feel intensely motivated, purposeful, and driven. The desperately desired version of tomorrow *will be* fulfilled.

Anthony—"Make her love me"

Anthony was gripped by a consuming obsession for his rejecting girl-friend, Cher, who, he thought, was beginning an affair with a younger, handsome colleague. Yet Anthony was convinced this woman was still only just beyond his reach. With the therapist's help, Cher *would* be restored to him. This fantasy of the beloved was far more real than Cher's actual flawed personality. It was a living vision which success-fully swamped the day-to- day contradictory reality of Cher's chilly behaviour towards Anthony. In the meanwhile, in the immediate present, Anthony had left his devoted wife and children to be near the beloved, where he also found himself unable to concentrate on his demanding legal work and court cases.

Anthony was seldom interested in the therapist's interventions. He would pause to listen politely and patiently before returning to his task of bending harsh reality to fit his projected vision. Time was in the witness box and would crack under the right pressure. The therapist existed solely to bolster the fantasy and to make the wish come true. Although the focus of "This year" and "Next year" states are contrast-ing, as with Beth, behind Anthony's conscious, driven desire was the underlying infant yearning for loving parents—a similar "unconscious wish magically to turn the clock back and be a baby" (Ledermann, 1989, p. 108).

But with Anthony the therapist could not make any dent in the patient's transference to his fantasy of Cher, which filled all the space (cf. Peters, 1991, pp. 77–92). Only *Cher* could function as the ideal infancy parent. Anthony's feelings towards the therapist were as for a benign fairy godfather, who was taking far too long to deliver the transformation scene.

Anthony implored the therapist himself to arrange to see Cher, to convince her that "I know Cher better than any other man has known her—and we are so compatible . . . that she *should* come back to me."

The therapist responded: "*You* would be wanting me to make her love you. And *I* would want to be encouraging her to leave you . . . Maybe I *would* make her love you *if* I were your fairy godfather, but I am not . . ."

This response illustrates the tightrope the therapist walked between containment of the obsessional "Next year" fantasy. He was attempting both to soften the harshness of the real "I would want to encourage her to leave you" with the illusory, *fantasy* tense of "I *would* make her love you if I were your fairy godfather".

Later, a more direct and unambiguous dose of reality was introduced when Anthony declared, "I love Cher so much, there is nothing in the world I wouldn't do for her. So surely she owes *something* to me." The therapist commented that it was not true that the patient would do anything in the world for Cher, who seemed to want only one thing from Anthony: to be left alone by him.

However, nothing daunted by such plain-speaking, the patient's tenacity in bending the future to his will slowly paid off, for in a sense, he did "make Cher love him" in that Cher agreed to see Anthony once a week for sex. The barrister seemed to have won his case.

But once that original desired future became, in some measure, actualised, Anthony was unable to fully savour his time with Cher and continued to focus only on the future: "Why am I so depressed? Always fearing that she won't come next time and that she won't ever really love me after all? . . ."

CHAPTER SIXTEEN

Sometime: the past and the future perfect

"When a spider spins its web, does it not cast the main threads ahead of itself, and then follow along them from behind?"

(Hillesum, 1999, p. 356).

To be in a "Sometime" state is to be mired in fantasies which stretch back to remembered and unremembered disturbances, and stretch forward to the end of life or even beyond. Attachment to an indelible past welded to the spurious certainty and seduction of the future perfect, "what *will* have been", proves irresistible. For those in a "Sometime" state, this fantasy tense modifies and displaces the grimness of the immediate present. It recalls the memorable line in Beckett's *Happy Days,* when Winnie, immobilized, buried up to her neck in sand, chirps to her equally immobilized, silent spouse, Willie, "It *will have been* a happy day."

This fantasy time is a way of vaulting right over time's natural unfolding to an imagined temporal position, where not only are all present pains and plans perfected—completed—but also, from this all-seeing perspective, the *future* is felt to be already safely behind the bars of the all-knowing, all-seeing "Sometime" dweller. The future is "over" and wrapped up. From the perspective of "what will have been", all one's time allocation has been compressed, rolled up into a little ball. In reneging on human limits and adopting an omnipotent position—God's vantage point—the future perfect is the most audacious and potent tense. Yet this compression of all time cannot save the subject from operating in a temporal mode because the future perfect is, of course, still conceived from the standpoint of the inescapable *now*.

For those existing in a "Sometime" state, their presenting dilemma often seems to arise from adolescent crises over identity, sexual and existential. The persistent wounds of that earlier phase have interfered with the formation of adult relationships and with confidence in both sexual and creative powers. The earlier disturbance casts its shadow over all later living, so that *"Sometime"* in the form of "What will have been" can even precipitate one's existence beyond the grave.

Such "Sometime" states appear associated with a particular sense of "not enoughness" in terms of worth, talent, experience. For this deficit, the individual feels shamefully responsible. As well as the familiar deprivations of too little love and affirmation, this lack often takes the form of *not having had enough* sexual experience to be worthy of respect, especially by oneself. It is less a craving for the live experience of sex in the present, than desiring the lifeless trophy of *having had* "enough" to have earned one's colours in the world, to be deemed a valid being. As suggested in the following illustrations, this "will have been" goes well beyond attempts to shape and control merely the immediate future.

"She loves her mummy"

Mirella, attractive, in her early thirties, was trapped by a long-ended teenage love affair that haunted and prevented her from forming other relationships. She felt despised and pitied by friends and family who could all, as she put it, "boast success in the relationship department". One reason for her failure to "move on", she believed, was her "obesity". "I don't suffer from body dysmorphia. I am just disgustingly gross," she stoutly declared. Her therapist grew anxious, for, at five foot nine inches, Mirella weighed in at around eight stone.

On public transport and in public places she dreaded being stared at, always skulking along, enveloped in "my cloak of invisibility". When the therapist pointed out that the eyes of another can't physically hurt, and also that behind Mirella's obsessive terror of people's eyes might lie a desire or need for them, she responded irritably. "You're telling me that *physical* pain is the worst thing. Well, I'm telling you that's a fallacy! Eyes do hurt, words do hurt, far, far more than sticks and stones!" She was quiet for a moment, unusually pensive, coming up with a—for *her*—pleasurable, if rather ominous association: "I've never thought of this till now, but I do remember how my mother always used to hold me on her lap. She would hug me tightly and rock me, gazing into my eyes and singing over and over the same words, never varying them, 'She loves her mummy. She loves her mummy. She loves her mummy.' I loved her doing this. These were the only words she ever sang to me and I could always get comfort from hearing them in my head."

A comfort derived from such swamping, one-sided activity sounds more like *cold* comfort. And Mirella's mode of escaping from her past-haunted present was also a kind of cold comfort, which took the form of a lugubrious focusing on the future perfect. "Mine *will have been* an empty life. My teenage boyfriend *will have had* a partner, children and grandchildren. Those future offspring ought to have been *my* descendants. They should have attended *my* funeral and mourned *my* death.

During the therapy, matters got worse with Mirella. She began to feel an extreme dread of going to work and was plagued by alarming panic attacks, hiding in the toilets for long stretches of time. The therapist feared she was on the verge of breaking down completely. In the midst of this despair, one day Mirella mentioned in passing that her father had got stall tickets for a week-long dance festival. "I *would have* loved to go," she confessed, as if it was too late and the entire event were already over. Yet her whole demeanour seemed to change. Her voice became more alive and expressive and the therapist commented that this was the first time she had heard Mirella mention dance. "Oh yes," she replied. "Dance is my great passion. I wish I could have gone to that festival. But of course I couldn't." "Why?" demanded the therapist. "Surely it's obvious! Why do you think I gave up my dance training in the first place?" She gave the somewhat bemused therapist no time to answer, continuing, "How could I go on being seen among all those perfect bodies, making mine appear still more obscene? . . . Anyway, I couldn't get time off work."

The therapist reflected; "But at the festival you will be *seeing* more than being seen. You must go! You must get sick leave from work."

Mirella was quite struck by this unusual coercion and to the therapist's surprise, although not taking the path of sick leave, she used up her holiday times and nerved herself to attend the festival protected by the "cloak" of her father. Having survived this ordeal of visibility among the beautiful ones, Mirella felt convinced that the experience had averted a full breakdown. Watching others engaged in her beloved but forbidden pursuit for a whole week drew her gaze away from herself, restoring it to a less distorted, less desperate perspective.

As her illness abated and the primitive persecutory anxieties began to lessen, Mirella burnt all the long-treasured letters and mementoes from her teenage relationship and took the step of moving away from the sweetheart's area. She is considering the possibility of *one day* enrolling for a Performing Arts course, where dance would be a component. Instead of staying frozen in the past and the future perfect, she is beginning to dwell in the present and to link with a potential future.

Juliet: "my pot of poison"

Juliet, a young Hindu woman, was treated as a slave by her busy professional parents from an early age. When she was nine a baby brother was born. For his total care the grandmother was brought in. Not only was this grandmother crazily possessive of the brother but she banned Juliet from all access to him, so Juliet became convinced that she herself was contaminated.

Her miserable life changed with the development, in her teens, of a passionate relationship with a Sikh boy by whom she twice became pregnant and had two abortions. Upon the death of her oppressive father Juliet was now free to marry her Romeo. But she asked him to wait for two months so that she could properly mourn her father. At the end of that time she learned that *his* parents had intervened and married him off to a young Sikh girl.

Prior to therapy, Juliet had made one suicide attempt and, following this blow, she was now contemplating another. Startlingly, this young girl said to her therapist: "My husband and children are dead. I am old and waiting to die. I shall grind up my pot of poison and swallow it."

By a strange but understandable contortion, it seemed that Juliet had in fantasy simultaneously jumped forward into the distant future of her old age and also back into her youthful past, to compose for herself in the *present* the identity of an old crone. This persona/mask acted as a protection from the pressures of that present. But the means were sinister. For Juliet had so fully introjected the bad grandmother/witch, become so wholly identified with her grandmother's perception of Juliet as bad, that she could now experience only self-destructive feelings towards herself. Her words were those of the grandmother/ventriloquist. She was just the doll.

As so frequently seen in psychotherapy, the patient was possessed by such a dominant persecutory "voice", that it was mistaken for the whole self. But if it can possibly be "unmasked" as an impostor, there is then the potential of a space opening up between the self and the invader. This unmasking is likely to be inseparable from unravelling the confusion of times so graphic in the case of Juliet.

Etty Hillesum: as if I had somehow been through it already

This "What will have been" is compelling, not only as a dangerous weapon or an evasive tool, but it can also be self-vindicating as an effective protection and resource in conditions of extremity. While the experience of both Raphael and Juliet exemplifies the dangers of evasively occupying this temporal position, its exploitation by the young visionary, Etty Hillesum, is an inspiring example. During the Holocaust, as a young, soon-to-die voluntary inmate of the horrific concentration camp in Westerbork, Holland, Hillesum was subjected to its moment-to-moment agonies and awaiting deportation to a destination that she knew would render her current hell a heaven. She was liberated by this "will have been" perspective in a creative and sanity-saving way. Not long before her inevitable death, she wrote to friends:

> I shall try to convey to you how I feel, but I am not sure if my metaphor is right. When a spider spins its web, does it not cast the main threads ahead of itself, and then follows along them from behind? The main path of my life stretches like a long journey before me and already reaches into another world. It is just as if

everything that happens here and that is still to happen were some- how discounted inside me. As if I had somehow been through it already, and was now helping to build a new and different society. [Hillesum, 1999, p. 356]

CHAPTER SEVENTEEN

Never

The child's toys and the old man's reasons
Are the fruits of the two seasons.

(William Blake, 1948, p. 120)

The question of memory

How well must the memory of the therapist function for the needs of the patient? How far does poor memory interfere with the process of creative playing and meaning-making? To approach each session "without memory and desire", as urged by Bion, is an important strand in psychotherapy, but equally true is, surely, that the therapist's remembering serves the patient as a main symbolic substitute for actual physical holding. Particularly for people in very fragile, insecure states, who have taken the risk of putting themselves in the hoped-for strong arms of the therapist, the therapist's remembering has a vital holding-together function. This holding-together is not just about the therapist's general picture or sense of a patient's particular patterning. The truth of an person lies in the detail of the pattern. For a fragmented person, the need "to be known in all his bits and pieces" (Winnicott, 1958, p. 150) may be a lowly need, but it may be what enables some patients to feel held and to carry on coming to sessions. "To be known means to feel integrated at least in the person of the analyst" (*ibid.*).

For the therapist to say, "Perhaps what *you* remember as important differs from what *I* remember as important" may serve as a reminder of separateness, but is not likely to promote the fullness of trust essential for progress. Just as the infant's continuity of being depends on the combined physical and psychological holding by the m/other, so the patient's going-on-being is aided by a sense of being held in the therapist's mind.

Winnicott viewed mistakes by the therapist as an unconscious response to the patient's own unconscious need for the point of original failure to materialize in the therapy. For some, the distress or anger aroused by the therapist's failure becomes a growing point. But for others, some forgettings prove disastrous and the patient may even leave the therapy because of just one lapse by the therapist. In any case, the therapist's poor memory is a traumatic way of learning that last month's, last week's, even yesterday's words were transient, provisional, dependent solely on a particular context, if not allegedly the product of the patient's own fallible memory, unconsciously invented.

The patient's recognition that some lapses may be more to do with the ageing of the therapist than her indifference does not prevent the dependent, vulnerable self from feeling dropped and uncared for. The question behind this statement is, therefore, how possible is it to be fully and meaningfully with another person, in the hope of growth and change, without the external packaging, the binding thread and security of conscious mutual remembering? If the patient's memories of the therapy are not validated, this can be experienced as a very real and primitive threat to his or her being.

The therapist also needs to be able to remember when the patient forgets. To approach a session with openness and without preconceptions is fine as long as she can simultaneously keep in her mind the threads that connect today's encounter with preceding ones. When the patient, suppressing earlier revealed aspects of himself, is exalted or crushed by today's mood, it is important for the therapist, whether aloud or silently, to recall and connect this state with the rest of the person she has already met, as well as those aspects she can so far only visualize.

Taking the issue of fading memory to its furthest extreme of splintered seconds: how far is it possible to incorporate the phenomenon of Alzheimer's disease, or at least, dementia, into concepts of the self, when there appears to be no longer a functioning self? Jungian analysts have recorded work with a patient who knew his terminal illness would bring about the loss of his faculties to the point of total mindlessness (Baker & Wheelwright, 1984, p. 256). Therapy with this person involved the gradual and graceful surrender of himself to the ravages upon his mind, so that somehow dignity remained in his accepting his loss of dignity. Similarly, Valerie Sinason presents a remarkable account of working in an unswerving Kleinian way with a philosophy don who realized that he was developing Alzheimer's, but the psychic pain became too unbearable for him to continue (Sinason, 1992, p. 87).

The contrast between a potential for recovery of both time's and the self's fullness, and the experience of those whose time has narrowed to fractured instants, is demonstrated in the following piece of work.

Cordelia: "What balloons?"

A young woman training as a a drama therapist was given a placement at a geriatric day centre. Cordelia soon learned that her struggles to form and run an ongoing group, as well as her hours of thoughtful planning, were a sheer waste of time. Each session had to be literally without memory and desire. There could be no continuity, no referring back, often no recognition of the therapist from one session to the next, although one old lady was persistently attacking and destructive towards Cordelia. Another member of the group would repeatedly interrupt with the same urgent question, which always had to be answered, "Where do I live?"

There could never be an entire, good session. The only reward would be rare, single, sealed-off moments without any before or after. Yet Cordelia knew that she would be sad to leave the placement—particularly to lose three of her clients, for whom she had developed a real fondness. Indeed, she was rather dreading the ending and farewells, which, inevitably, would be something of a non-event and she guessed she might feel a little cheated.

The last session began in the usual way, with members of the group complaining, "Why am I here? I don't want to be here." The session was structured around activities to do with saying goodbye, which led up to the therapist's announcing that today she and they were going to be saying goodbye to each other, as this was their last meeting. Immediately, the same old lady who had been so attacking burst into loud, inconsolable tears, sobbing that she *had* thought she had nothing else to lose. A normally very confused and withdrawn, silent woman crept over to the crying one, put her arm round her and began to sing, "We'll meet again", whereupon, to Cordelia's amazement, the rest of the group spontaneously joined in.

At the end, Cordelia distributed balloons that had the name of each member inscribed with coloured markers. These were then bunched together and hung up in the Group room, to everyone's apparent pleasure. A little later, during lunch in the dining room, the manager of the centre arrived, asking the clients about these balloons and they replied, "What balloons?" . . . For them, those balloons had already floated away from their minds. But for Cordelia, this ending was an unexpected gift.

This experience shows vividly how, without memory of the immediate past, or desire for the future, the present is destroyed before it can ever be adequately registered. There are no means of linking moments together. So being in the world here and now becomes a total mockery, a nightmare succession of broken up frag-ments in a perpetual fog. The occasion also underlines the terrify-ingly absolute inseparability between time and identity. While for the clients, there was neither time past nor time future, for Cordelia, the therapist, it was an initiation into the nature of the therapeutic challenge of maintaining continuity, and, when that fails, when there is nothing but *now*, of holding on to her clients with no conti-nuity at all. Everything is never.

CHAPTER EIGHTEEN

The who you dream yourself

For children, "the strongest appeal should be to the imagination, the power by which the child prises himelf free from
the present and loosens the clutch of the immediate. In the
imaginative act the child disengages himself from the partial
and broken, from 'the universe as a mass of little parts', and
comes to conceive of a larger unity and more inclusive
whole. The now is extended and the here complicated. The
pressure of the momentary is relaxed and the actual charged
with the possible"

(Walsh, *circa* 1968, p. 24)

Good time—with memory and desire

My thoughts

I sometimes wonder what my mind is like inside, often I fancy
that it is like this. I feel as if my mind goes round and round
like the earth and if my lessons make me think hard it begins
to spin. In my other class it was getting all stodgy and still and
lumpy and rusty. I feel as if there is a ball in my mind and it is
divided into pieces—each piece stands for a different mood. The

ball turns every now and then and that's what makes me change moods. I have my learning mood, my goodlooks mood, my happy mood, my loose-end mood and my grumpy mood, my misrable [*sic*] mood and my planning mood. At the moment I am writing this I am in my thoughtful mood. When I am in my thoughtful mood I think out my maths and plan stories and poems. When my kitten is in her thoughtful mood she thinks shall I pounce or not, and shall I go to sleep or not. This sort of thing goes on in my own mind too. It is very hard for me to put my thoughts into words. Sarah Gristwood aged 7. [McLeod, 1972, p. 9]

A child with such a developed power of written self-expression might well echo the often quoted words of another young girl, originally reported by E. M. Forster: "How can I know what I think until I see what I say?" It has, indeed, been provocatively argued by the post-structuralist, Jacques Derrida, that writing *precedes* speech. Certainly, if freely playing in the form of talking with and in the presence of another promotes growth and healing, there is a still greater freedom in talking to oneself in the initial privacy of the visible word. This child's writing shows untrammelled access to innermost, hitherto, unformed thoughts and feelings.

This inner scenario is an expression of integration, of roundedness. It shows an instinctive awareness of the mysterious multiplicity of the personality, of the many "moods" generated within one's seeming singleness. The child has the capacity to reflect upon herself as well as entering imaginatively into the mind of another with identification, with empathy. She possesses a highly developed ability to compare and contrast—to think metaphorically— and to make classifications. She can speculate, day-dream, and roam the tenses. This child's self is well enough, even superbly, held together in space–time by her advanced meaning-making powers and apparent emotional security.

"Good time", then, refers to this capacity for a balanced relationship between present, past, and future. Imagining possible futures is incorporated into the map of past and present, forging strong, binding temporal links. *Imagining* futures and *remembering* the past contrasts with the time-sick *fantasies* of the previous chapters. So the more conscious day-dreaming by Sarah Gristwood, above, in *My Thoughts*, rather than defensive and escapist, is growth-promoting, towards finding one's own distinct voice, one's desires and hopes, away from the clamour of parents and peers.

The role of the future in child development, particularly through playing, is confirmed by the psychologist, Vygotsky, who, echoing Freud (Freud, 1908e, pp. 141–153) asserts that the best point for reaching, teaching, stretching, a child is neither at a stage of unripeness, nor ripeness, but of *ripening*. He declares that

> In play, a child is *always beyond his average age,* above his daily behaviour, in play, it is as though he were a head taller than himself. As in the focus of a magnifying glass, play contains all developmental tendencies in a condensed form and is a major source of development. [Vygotsky, 1978, p. 102]

This *always beyond his average age,* with the child's imaginatively stretching himself, is caught in the following evocation of a young boy's day-dreaming during his underwater possession of a nearby river:

> Thoughts that were partly dreams slipped through his mind. Imperial, childish dreams. The mild river fostered them as school and home never did. Brittle, boy's bones stretched in a flash to the shape and substance of a man; his child's mind—bigoted and unsteady—was great with the sum of wisdom; fame, honour, wealth, were all got as glibly as prizes in a fair. [Barker, 2003, p. 7]

Also encapsulated in "bigoted and unsteady, . . . great with the sum of wisdom; fame, honour, wealth, all got as glibly as prizes in a fair" is the gulf between a child's purposeful imagining the future and its potential adult realization. The future which *does not* exist here, now, is a loose cannon. As implied in the portrayal of this scene, planning, day-dreaming, hope, all these, even for a well-adjusted child, are fraught with potential perils.

How much more, then, must this gulf apply to damaged and disturbed children. But as testified by contemporary analytic writers, notably Anne Alvarez, what has proved a major shift of emphasis in their treatment, as well as attention to *fears* associated with past trauma, is the acknowledgement and incorporation of the *prospective*, of hope, of the vital concept of destiny, as signalled in imaginative day-dreaming. So it is crucial that the child "grows

within itself an imagined human figure of various degrees of recep-
tivity, friendship or enmity" (Alvarez, 1992, p. 25). For a hopeful
looking ahead, the individual needs to imagine himself or herself
as perceived and *thought* about by the other, and to "find himself in
the other" (Fonagy, 1995, p. 576). The title of Alvarez's book, *Live
Company*, refers, further, to the abundance, the plurality, of imagined figures (or internal objects) beyond the single mirroring
m/other of early infancy, needed for self-security. For roundedness,
"live company" must include the accommodation of ill-disposed as
well as favourably disposed figures.

For a child whose whole self must be carried by the therapist
(Alvarez, 1992, p. 13ff) as in the case of her long-term autistic
patient, Robbie, the orthodox belief in disillusionment and frustration as growth-promoting is simply not applicable. The child who
has not yet discovered "presence" will hardly benefit from the
pangs of absence. For such children, (indeed, might we not say, for
everybody?), "the object's *availability* can be as alerting and thought
provoking . . . as its *unavailability* in the less deprived child" (*ibid.*,
p. 163).

Hope and a sense of destiny are thus seen as inextricably intertwined with the "live company" of inner and outer relationships.
The inseparability between facing forwards in hope, "live
company" and therapeutic affirmation, rather than therapeutic
abstention, is illustrated by Alvarez in her account of a therapist's
clinical approach with a depressed boy. At first, the therapist sensi-
tively attunes to the boy's mood up to the point where he does a
drawing of a Super dream-car, which possesses all the amenities of
a richly furnished house and swimming pool. The boy "wished it
was his, he would never have to leave it for anything. You could
swim all day in the holidays" (*ibid.*, p. 121ff). Alvarez notes that the
therapist interpreted the boy's fantasy as a defence against separation from her. On hearing this observation, the boy seemed to
deflate. From then, the session sank further and Alvarez comments
that just as the child had begun to flower in the therapist's sensitive
understanding, the sun stopped shining. For the boy needed to hear
not that his fantasy could not be fulfilled, but that indeed his *very
experience of this desire was itself its fulfilment*: "he was not wishing
for, but had in fact found a spacious and available object in her"
[the therapist] (*ibid.*, p. 123).

The advent of such hope embodied in the fantasy, however unlikely its gratification in reality, nevertheless potentially transforms the quality of the boy's "now". Alvarez argues further that with many patients there may be a vital stage of helping them to *forget* the past in order to recover the present and conceptualize a future. As her comments on the fantasy of the Super car illustrate, fostering a less reductive and more teleological approach in responding to a patient's disclosures focuses on drawing out the implicit hope rather than the implicit fear.

In classical analytic writings, as Alvarez acknowledges, it is Jung who explicitly incorporates a focus on destiny as crucial for psychic health. For Jung, this focus is formed by the opposition between "those far seeing dreams or images which appear before the soul of the child, shaping his whole destiny" and the "profoundly primitive nature of the newborn infant and his highly differentiated inheritance" (Jung, 1928, p. 98).

By linking images, dreams and destiny, Jung recognizes that both asleep-dreaming and daydreaming, in forging strong temporal links, assist in the consolidation of the self.

The telling of asleep dreams

To imagine oneself as perceived and thought about by others, combined with the act of speaking in the presence of another and the experience of hearing both oneself and the other in this act (cf. Chapter Two), all are key factors no less in meaning-making while asleep than in awake meaning-making. Those involved with children—teachers, playworkers, parents, and the children themselves, as well as child therapists—testify to the collective and individual benefit of dream telling, whether in the intensity of a one-to-one psychotherapy set-up, or in looser, dream-sharing situations. Particularly in those cultures where people take for granted a more multi-dimensional world of dreams and spirits, as evoked in the writings of Jung, dream-telling plays an essential part in family life and childhood.

Such activity is an implicit recognition that the asleep and dreaming self is an integral part of the personality. Yet although this is quite widely acknowledged, like any other aspect of the human organism that withers through lack of use, for dreaming to act as a vital resource, the potential for dream telling needs to be fostered.

What, then, is happening in the experience of telling a dream? What is the nature of the exchange and the climate it creates? For the telling can be frustrating—the dream difficult to remember, fragmented. It can be hard to recapture the original *flavour*, and hard to face the self-exposure. Yet the urge to tell is almost invariably greater than the reluctance, with the relief and satisfaction in the telling and being heard—not least when speaking of nightmares. For telling is an act of trust, which can strengthen ties between dreamer and listener. Further, as so vividly testified in Jung's and countless other analytic writings, the telling may lead to an indication of the subject's unconscious hopes, fears, and anxieties for the future, as well as her unconscious captivity in the past.

The benefit of telling asleep dreams and also the vulnerability of the sleeper emerged in a single dream-session among a group of Local Authority playworkers. They spoke of their own dreams and of dreams related by children. It was reported that one child had been *forbidden to dream* because she was "beaten awake" by her parents if she screamed during a nightmare. In this confessional atmosphere of dream sharing, one member spoke for the first time of how, as a young boy, he used to sleepwalk into all the bedrooms, switching on every light until, finding his sister, he would take hold of her hand and she would lead him safely back to bed. Now, so many years later, he disclosed that he had been sexually abused by his father during those years. Although this fragment does not exactly qualify as a dream, it points to the value of an appreciative, dream-conscious climate. Another striking example illustrating the potential of the very concept of dreams came from the playworker whose attentive listening had alerted her to a child's presenting his unbearable real-life experiences *in the guise of a dream*. He could thus shelter behind the pretend dream format both to conceal from, and communicate to, the adult that these appalling things had, in reality, *happened* to him.

In this single session on dreams, the focus was less on the meaning and content of dreams and more on the nature of the exchange and the climate it creates. The telling of dreams belongs primarily to the relationship with the listener. It is rooted in transference and the heightening of transference. Such potency indicates the distinction between what can be done in one-to-one therapy and what is appropriate or possible for playworkers, teachers and others in the outside world.

The distinction between these roles was illustrated by the group's response to one playworker's recurring, pre-marital dream of reaching the altar on her wedding day on the arm of her bridegroom, only to find that this altar was on the edge of a swimming pool into which she immediately plunged. For this group dream-sharing, it seemed more appropriate to focus on what the experience of such a shock *felt like* than to encourage exploration of the deeper *meaning of the dream*. However, in practice, such distinctions may dissolve and indeed, the mere communication of such personal experiences to another may be more powerful than any "deeper" analysis. What matters then, is the perception and sensitivity of the listener, who needs to be alert to the manifold possibilities: one significant resource for the playworker is that, presumably unlike both therapists and teachers, playworkers are more free, because more fully *beside* the children, to initiate the topic of dreams by introducing a dream of their own.

Of further importance for the playworkers was their recognition of how the dimension of dreaming could stimulate and enrich the activities of art, drama, movement, and creative writing. There seemed to be a two-way process where the success or effectiveness of these projects owed much to the imaginative transformation of material into the substance of dreams. For example, there was the "poetry machine" and the summer holiday project where the play centre spread out into the surrounding town, exemplifying Winnicott's claim that asleep dreams are a richer imaginative source than the activity of daydreaming, however valid a part that may also have.

"A monster ate my teacher"

A barely four year old boy, who had enjoyed his first day at "big school", had assumed this first day also would be his last day at school. He was bitterly upset at having to go back tomorrow. During the night, he climbed sobbing into his parents' bed, settling straight back to sleep. Next day, the parents asked their son if he had been woken last night by a bad dream and the boy recalled that a monster had been gobbling up his teacher. Then, instead of resisting his second day at school, he hurried in eagerly, to inform his teacher of the dream.

Whatever may have been the teacher's unrecorded response to his pupil's news, is perhaps less important than the steps leading up to it: the child's expectation and reliance on his mother's and father's immediate soothing from his nightmare; their later inviting him to recount it, bringing the dream to the child's consciousness. For dreaming and the telling of dreams plays a part in the processing and management of reality. By a double transformation, the substance of reality is converted to the dream of the monster eating the teacher, which in turn transforms and makes palatable that reality—without any overt mention of the dream's possible meanings. For the meaning is in the process. The act of telling the dream and its being heard by the parents impelled their child to report it to the subject of the dream: his teacher. He became willing, after all, to try school for a second day—and, maybe for tomorrow and tomorrow and tomorrow.

*   *   *

In this final chapter, my focus has widened from the enclosed spaces of theatre and therapy to being in the outside world, with the dimension of dreams and the telling of dreams seen as strengthening the capacity to be securely embodied in one's time. For the child dreamer whose teacher was eaten by a monster and for the child writer of *My Thoughts,* this seems a good enough world for psychological growth, where playing and interpretation spring from a centred, aware self.

But those, like the children described by Anne Alvarez, for whom this world is perilous and disruptive, might need to be helped towards free playing and self-expression. Such help might include a more enclosed setting and the prop of structured games to foster a sense of self in time and space. For example, Winnicott's Squiggle Game facilitates freedom of expression within a simple set format, loosening the patient's tongue and providing for Winnicott a short cut to his/her unconscious thoughts and feelings. And in his Spatula Game with infants, any arbitrary distinction between "games" and "playing" dissolves in the discoveries yielded by the beautiful simplicity of "Observation of infants in a set situation" (Winnicott, 1958, p. 52).

In furthering a clearer sense of identity and imaginative awakening, Winnicott is willing to seize on any scraps available for the convergence of games and playing. When his fantasying, out-of-time patient, discussed in Chapter Twelve, complains of being stuck in her endless solitary card games, saying that "playing patience is a quagmire", he agrees that indeed such an actual *game* is a dead end, but adds that a corresponding *dream* of the game could be interpreted as, for example, "the self playing with God" (Winnicott, 1971, p. 36). Simply by conjuring with the patient's reference to a card game and pulling out a suggested dream, he appeals to her hidden more creative self, lifting her out of the "quagmire" that stops her from being in the world, here, now.

And in the episode between Pip and Miss Havisham, (mentioned in Chapter Five), Pip, panicking at the command, "Play, boy, play!" is then saved by the advent of Estella and the ensuing game of cards.

In the following final sequence, solitary regressive activity, card games and board games with the therapist join together in helping a deprived child, Maisie, towards playing. Maisie, aged thirteen, had been grossly abused and neglected, batted like a ping-pong ball between her parents. At a Play Centre, she saw a therapist for regular sessions, but otherwise, had no heart for any of the inviting activities at the Centre. Equally outside Maisie's present interest were the range of art materials: the clay, the beads, the face-painting, the collage. Neither would she have her face painted as a wolf, fox or other predator, which were the most popular choices for creative play and drama. And she would not be found in the kitchen area, where children were supervised in cooking a range of multi-cultural snacks, from Egyptian biscuits to chapatis.

It might be assumed that Maisie would have felt such activities were too babyish for her, but instead, Maisie spent much of her time in the soft-cushion area—a space filled entirely with cushions of various kinds and materials, originally designed for toddlers. Here Maisie could surrender to a regressive, tactile experience, which did not demand that she be focused or integrated in any way. The cushions answered the need for something in the world to a offer a sensual, holding experience similar to that enjoyed by the patient on the couch of the therapy room. In her therapy sessions, Maisie also played for long periods with the sand and water.

In the sand and water play and in her visits to the soft cushion area, perhaps Maisie was seeking to recreate the experience of infancy transitional states, where the sensual satisfactions of something other than the real-life mother—the cushions, sand and water—also evoked some primordial "good mother". Further meaning was given to her playing in this way by the proximity and availability of the therapist and their dawning relationship.

But the only playing with the therapist that Maisie could manage was of a tightly structured nature. She would, in total silence, engage in card games with her therapist. For card games were the only form of contact that used to occur between Maisie and her mother. In providing the security of one clear step at a time, these card games gave Maisie a structure and a form of holding. As yet she could neither speak nor play freely with her therapist, though eventually, as well as the silent card games, Maisie began also to join in *Snakes and Ladders* with the therapist. Then, at last, she began to talk. For whenever, to her annoyance, the dice forced Maisie's counter down a snake, her own tongue was loosened and she became able to express to the therapist, in most juicy terms, her pain and fury towards her mother. In the presence of the listening therapist, engrossed in the outcome of the game, Maisie was discovering also that the time and "the space of play is not teleological" (Kotowicz, 1997, p. 145).

REFERENCES

Alvarez, A. (1992). *Live Company*. London: Routledge.

Baker, B., & Wheelwright, J. (1984). Analysis with the aged. In: M. Stein (Ed.), *Jungian Analysis*. Boulder and London: Shambhala.

Balint, M. (1959). *The Regressed Patient and His Analyst*. (Third Annual Frieda Fromm-Reichmann Memorial Lecture).

Balint, M. (1979). *The Basic Fault*. London: Tavistock.

Barker, A. L. (2003). *Submerged*. London: Virago.

Barrett, W. (1978). Heidegger. In: B. Magee (Ed.), *Men of Ideas*. London: BBC.

Bate, J. (2003). Review of *Looking for Spinoza: Joy, Sorrow and the Feeling Brain*, by Antonio Damasio. The *Guardian*, 24 May.

Belsey, C. (2002). *Poststructuralism—A Very Short Introduction*. Oxford: Oxford University Press.

Blake, P. (2001). Think outside, not inside. In: J. Edwards, (Ed.), *Being Alive*. Sussex: Brunner-Routledge.

Blake, W. (1948). *Poetry and Prose of William Blake*. G. Keynes (Ed.). London: Nonesuch Press.

Bollas, C. (1987). *The Shadow of the Object*. London: Free Associations.

Bowie, M. (1982). Jacques Lacan. In: J. Sturrock (Ed.), *Structuralism and Since*. Oxford: Oxford University Press.

Brook, P. (1968). *The Empty Space*. Harmondsworth: Pelican.

Cousins, G. (1983). A note on mimesis. In: *Themes in Drama IV*. Harvard: Cambridge University Press.

Culler, J. (1983). *On Deconstruction*. London: Routledge.

Docker-Drysdale, B. (1991). *The Provision of Primary Experience*. New Jersey: Aronson.

Eagleton, T. (1983). *Literary Theory*. Oxford: Blackwell.

Elam, K. (1980). *The Semiotics of Theatre and Drama*. London: Methuen.

Evans, D. (1996). *An Introductory Dictionary of Lacanian Psychoanalysis*. London: Routledge.

Faladé, S. (1987). In: C. Mathelin (Ed.), *Lacanian Psychotherapy with Children*. New York: The Other Press, 1999.

Fonagy, P. (1995). Psychoanalysis, cognitive-analytic therapy, mind and self. *British Journal of Psychotherapy, 11*(4): 575–583.

Freud, S. (1908e). Creative writers and daydreaming. *S.E., 9*. London: Hogarth.

Freud, S. (1920g). Beyond the pleasure principle. *S.E., 18*. London: Hogarth.

Fuesil, R. (1981). *Themes in Drama*. Cambridge: Cambridge University Press.

Grotstein, J. (1997). One pilgrim's progress. In: T. Mintrani & A. Mintrani (Eds.), *Encounters with Autistic States*. London: Aronson.

Heidegger, M. (1980). In J. Miller (Ed.) *Men of Ideas*. London: BBC.

Hillesum, E. (1999). *An Interrupted Life: The Diaries and Letters of Etty Hillesum 1941–43*. London: Persephone Books.

Hillman, J. (1983). *Archetypal Psychology*. Dallas, TX: Spring Publications.

Hubback, J. (1988). *People Who Do Things to Each Other*. Wilnette, ILL: Chiron.

Huizinga, J. (1949). *Homo Ludens: a Study of the Play Element in Culture*. London: Routledge and Kegan Paul. Quoted in Farhi, (1991). "D. W. Winnicott and a personal tradition". In: L. Spurling (Ed.), *From the Words of my Mouth*. London: Routledge & Kegan Paul.

Jeffares, A. N. (Ed.) (1976). *W. B. Yeats, Selected Poetry*. London: Macmillan.

Jung, C. G. (1915). Letter to Hans Schmidt, 6 Nov 1915. In: Hayman: *A Life of Jung*. London: Bloomsbury, 1999.

Jung, C. G. (1928). The structure and dynamics of the psyche. In: *Collected Works*: 8. 1960–69.

Kotowicz, Z. (1997). *R. D. Laing and the Paths of Anti-Psychiatry*. London: Routledge.

Lacan, J. (1954). *Ecrits: A Selection*. A. Sheridan (Trans.). New York: Norton, 1977.

Lacan, J. (1960a). *Seminaire, Livre V111. Le Transfert*. Paris: Seuil, 1991.

Lacan, J. (1964). *The Seminar. Book XI. The Four Fundamental Concepts of Psychoanalysis*. A. Sheridan (Trans.). London: Hogarth Press and Institute of Psychoanalysis, 1977.

Lacan, J. (1975). Geneva lecture. In: C. Mathelin (Ed.), *Lacanian Psychotherapy with Children*. New York: The Other Press, 1999.

Lacan, J. (1982). In: J. Sturrock (Ed.), *Structuralism and Since*. Oxford: Oxford University Press.

Langer, S. (1942). *Philosophy in a New Key*. Cambridge: Harvard University Press, 1974.

Leavy, S. (1983). The image and the word. In: Smith and Kerrigan (Eds.), *Interpreting Lacan*: New Haven and London: Yale University Press.

Ledermann, R. (1989). Narcissistic disorder and its treatment. In: A. Samuels (Ed.), *Psychopathology—Contemporary Jungian Perspectives*. London: Karnac.

Levinas, E. (1993). *The Levinas Reader*. S. Hand (Ed.), Oxford: Blackwell.

McLeod, A. (Ed.) (1972). "My thoughts", by Sarah Gristwood. In: *Openings: Penguin English Projects, Stage Two*. Harmondsworth: Penguin.

Maiello, S. (1997). Going beyond. In: T. Mintrani & A. Mintrani (Eds.), *Encounters with Autistic States*. London: Jason Aronson.

Mannoni, M. (1987). *The Child, His "Illness" and the Others*. London: Karnac.

Mathelin, C. (Ed.) (1999). *Lacanian Psychotherapy with Children*. New Haven: Yale University Press.

Meltzer, D. (1992). *The Claustrum*. Strath Tey, Perthshire: The Clunie Press.

Milner, M. (1952). The role of illusion in symbol formation. In: *The Suppressed Madness of Sane Men*. London: Routledge, 1998.

Moggach, D. (2004). *These Foolish Things*. London: Chatto and Windus.

Pessoa, F. (1935). *Selected Poems*. J. Griffin (Trans.). Harmondsworth: Penguin, 1986.

Pessoa, F. (1935). *The Surprise of Being*. J. Greene & A. Mafra (Trans.). London: Angel Books, 1986.

Peters, R. (1991). The therapist's expectation of the transference. *Journal of Analytical Psychology, 36*: 77–92.

Richards, V. (1993). Time-sickness. *Winnicott Sudies, 8*.

Richards, V. (1994). Mothers, mirrors and masks. *Winnicott Sudies, 9*.

Richards, V. (1996). *The Person Who Is Me*. London: Karnac.

Richards, V. (2002). In: D. Barford (Ed.), *The Ship of Thought: Essays on Psychoanalysis and Learning*. London: Karnac.

Rousseau, J. (1997). In: J. Culler (Ed.), *Literary Theory: A Very Short Introduction*. Oxford: Oxford University Press.

Sass, L. A. (1996). *The Paradoxes of Delusion*. USA: Cornell University Press. Quoted in review by Ian Mcgilchrist in *London Review of Books, circa* 1996.

Sechehaye, M. A. (1951). *Symbolic Realisation*. New York: International Universities Press, 1970.

Segal, H. (1983). Melanie Klein. In: J. Miller (Ed.), *States of Mind*. London: BBC.

Sinason, V. (1992). The man who was losing his brain. In: *Mental Handicap and the Human Condition*. London: Free Association Books.

Stanislavsky, C. (1950). *Building a Character*. London: Methuen, 1979.

Steiner, G. (1978). *Heidegger*. Sussex: The Harvester Press.

Strawson, G. (2002). The mind's I. The *Guardian*, 23 November. Guardian Unlimite@Guardian Newspapers Limited 2002.

Strawson, G. (2003). Review of *The Ethics of Memory* by Avishai Margalit. The *Guardian*, 4 January. Unlimite@Guardian Newspapers Limited 2003.

Strindberg, A. (1955). Preface to a "A Dream Play" In: *Six Plays of Strindberg*. E. Sprigg (Trans.). USA: Anthor.

Sturrock, J. (Ed.) (1982). Introduction. In: *Structuralism and Since*. Oxford: Oxford University Press.

Swerling, A. (1971). *Strindberg's Impact in France 1920–1960*. Cambridge: Trinity Lane Press.

Tustin, F. (1986). *Autistic Barriers in Neurotic Patients*. London: Karnac.

Umbert, E. (1988). *C. G. Jung*. USA: Chiron.

Unterecker, L. (1979). *A Reader's Guide to the Work of W. B. Yeats*. New York: Thames and Hudson.

Veltrusky, J. (1940). (Trans.) Man and object in the theater. Quoted in: Elam, K. *The Semiotics of Theatre and Drama*. London: Methuen, 1980.

Vygotsky, L. (1934). *Thought and Language*. London: MIT Press, 2000.

Vygotsky, L. (1978). Quoted in Alvarez, A. *Live Company*, London: Routledge, 1992.

Walsh, W. (c. 1968). *Use of the Imagination*. Harmondsworth: Pelican:, 1980.

Winnicott, D. W. (1958) *Through Paediatrics to Psychoanalysis*. London: Tavistock [reprinted London: Hogarth Press, 1987].

Winnicott, D. W. (1965). *The Maturational Processes and the Facilitating Environment*. London: Hogarth Press [reprinted London: Karnac 1992).

Winnicott, D. W. (1971). *Playing and Reality*. London: Routledge, 1996.

Winnicott. D. W. (1986). *Holding and Interpretation*. London: Hogarth Press, 1986.

Winnicott, D. W. (1989). *Psychoanalytic Explorations*, London: Karnac (quoted in Richards, V., *The Person Who is Me*, London, Karnac, 1996).

Wright, E. (1984). *Psychoanalytic Criticism, Theory in Practice*. London: Methuen.

Yeats, W. B. (1935). *The Collected Poems of W. B. Yeats*. London: Macmillan, 1973.

Yeats, W. B. (1939). *Selected Plays of W. B. Yeats*. London: Macmillan, 1982.

INDEX